My Mind on Trial

Books by Eugen Loebl

Mental Work: The True Source of Wealth

Stalinism in Prague

Die intellektuelle Revolution
(published in Germany and Austria)

Conversations with the Bewildered

Marxismus: Wegweiser und Irrweg
(published in Germany and Austria)

Humanomics

My Mind on Trial

Eugen Loebl

My Mind on Trial

A Harvest/HBJ Book

A Helen and Kurt Wolff Book

Harcourt Brace Jovanovich

New York and London

Printed in the United States of America

Library of Congress Cataloging in Publication Data

Loebl, Eugen, 1907–
My mind on trial.

(A Harvest/HBJ book)
"A Helen and Kurt Wolff book."
1. Loebl, Eugen. 2. Political prisoners—
Czechoslovakia—Biography. I. Title.
DB217.L63A35   1976b   364.1'3   77-16098
ISBN 0-15-663800-2

First Harvest/HBJ edition 1978

A B C D E F G H I J

For my son, Ivan

Contents

Historical Note

Czechoslovakia, now the Czecho-Slovak Socialist Republic, was established in 1918 by Czechs and Slovaks, from territories formerly part of the Austro-Hungarian Empire. Within its borders were a sizable German minority, the Sudetendeutschen, who were encouraged by Hitler's Germany to demand autonomy. This led to a crisis, culminating in the notorious Munich Pact of September 30, 1938, in which Czechoslovakia as originally constituted was dismembered. Six months later, in March 1939, German troops occupied what remained of the country, which became the German protectorate of Bohemia and Moravia. Eduard Beneš, who had resigned as president in 1938, resumed the title and fled to England. He appointed a coalition government and political advisory board (called the State Council) from the supporters who had accompanied him. Although there were no Communists in the government, some Communists did become members of the State Council in 1943. After World War II, Czechoslovakia was reconstituted as a democratic republic, with close economic ties to the Soviet Union. A Communist coup in February 1948 placed the country under Communist rule and virtually under Soviet domination. There was an attempt to liberalize and humanize the system, known to the world as the "Prague Spring" and initiated by party secretary Alexander Dubcek, a Slovak, but this was crushed in August 1968 by a Soviet invasion.

Acknowledgments

The events described in this book took place as much as a quarter of a century ago. The task of reconstructing the years of my arrest and imprisonment was a difficult and often tedious one. Returning to the bits and pieces of my experiences during those years, I felt like a stamp collector faced with a large but long-neglected collection. A good deal of sorting, weeding out, and cataloguing had to be done before my "collection" could be put in any reasonable order and sequence. Fortunately, I had the help of a former student and research assistant, James Stark. Over many months, we discussed those years, and the transcription of these discussions served as gridwork and essential raw material for my book. For his tireless dedication to a grueling task I want to express my gratitude.

I was also fortunate in having the assistance of a fellow countryman who had himself lived through the period described in this book and knew me well. His informed questions helped to evoke those gray areas one tends to repress because of the pain and guilt they reawaken. His editing and writing experience helped greatly to bring the manuscript into focus. I take this opportunity to express my gratitude, while respecting his desire to remain anonymous.

I want to thank Greta, my wife, whose great sensitivity and understanding helped me to gain better insight into myself.

My Mind on Trial

Washington, D.C.

My mission in Washington was rather delicate. I was the Czechoslovak first deputy minister of foreign trade, and the Politburo—the ruling body of the Communist party of Czechoslovakia—had sent me to America to try to warm up the cold war.

It was 1949, and the climate was not exactly propitious for such a venture. On the Socialist side, the Yugoslav Tito had just been cast out of the Communist bloc, and Stalin had condemned him for deviation and heresy. In China, a victorious Mao Tse-tung was sweeping the remnants of the regime of the "renegade bourgeois fascist" Chiang Kai-shek into the sea. The doctrine of ceaseless class war had just been proclaimed; Stalin said that the greater the triumphs of the world proletariat, the stronger would be the resistance of the wounded imperialists and the greater would be their hatred of the victorious world revolution.

In the United States, under President Harry Truman, a policy of containment of Communism had been adopted. The Hiss trials were in full swing. Indeed, not a very good climate for sensitive negotiations.

Only a year before, in February of 1948, the Communist party of Czechoslovakia had seized the reins of the government after a misfired pre-emptive strike by the liberals. There was no bloodshed, and the Communists were astonished at the ease with which the take-over was accomplished. Not only was the party well organized; it also had a plurality—forty-two percent—in the 1946 election. After Munich and their terrible experience in

World War II, even those Czechs and Slovaks who were not so keen on the nationalization of industry saw in the Soviet Union a solid guarantee that the resurgence of a Nazi movement would be impossible in the future.

The United States government had reacted to the establishment of a Communist regime by stopping exports of all equipment and materials that they thought could be used for military purposes. We had already ordered and paid for something like thirty-five or forty million dollars' worth of equipment for a tire factory, a steel mill, and mines. These materials were actually being loaded when the embargo was put into effect. Without the export permission, we had to put the equipment in storage and pay a steep bill—one hundred thousand dollars a month—a lot of money for an impoverished country like Czechoslovakia in 1949.

And that was only the beginning. The cold war was growing colder, and members of the Czechoslovak embassy in the United States were treated as if they had measles. Nobody invited them anywhere, and they were snubbed even by neutrals. Their only company was the very small circle of other Socialist diplomats, who did not dare offer much solace to one another. With the Berlin blockade beginning and Tito's defection already smoldering, the diplomat of a Socialist country had the uneasy feeling that any step he might take or any phrase he might utter could be condemned as a mistake or a deviation.

When I arrived in Washington, I found the Czechoslovak Ambassador, Dr. Vladimir Outrata, in deep depression. He had originally been a university professor and had written several books on Marxist history. When Outrata came to the White House to present his credentials, President Truman refused to shake hands with him, stood up from his desk, walked to the window, and studied the landscape while Outrata stumbled through his speech. The President did not even bother to turn around when Dr. Outrata had finished, and the flustered Ambassador had to hand over his papers to an aide.

Dr. Outrata and his wife were practically prisoners of the

embassy. They seldom went out, and they were afraid even to talk to each other except in highly loyal phrases, as they felt that their private apartment in the embassy might be bugged and reports sent to Prague about what they did and what they said.

He invited me to dinner, but we did not talk openly; he was fearful of microphones—American and Soviet as well as Czech ones—and so he spoke only about the theater, books, the cinema, abstract questions, and mutual acquaintances in Prague. The next morning, when we took a stroll through the garden, he finally relaxed and confessed that he did not know what to do in the situation facing him. He was worried that he might be called back to Prague and accused of incompetence.

I told Outrata not to worry. I had spoken with the Minister of Foreign Affairs, Vlado Clementis, who naturally knew that the strained relationship between the United States and Czechoslovakia had nothing to do with Outrata's competence. We all knew that the cold war had created a difficult and dangerous situation, and now our government, or, rather, the party leadership, had decided to try to change this situation and to create a new basis for our country's relationship to the West. This, I told Dr. Outrata, was the reason for my visit to the United States. He had not been briefed through the normal diplomatic channels because the details of my mission had to be kept an absolute secret.

I explained to him that now, with the party in complete power in Czechoslovakia, the threat that a closer relationship with the West, and with the United States in particular, could strengthen the non-Communist parties in our country no longer existed. In view of this, I had been entrusted by the Chairman of the party, President Klement Gottwald, to devise a plan that would bridge the gap between us and the West. My plan focused on our relationship with France, Great Britain, and the United States, and negotiations with the first two nations had turned out rather well. The key, however, was the agreements that could be reached with the United States.

We would offer the U.S. full compensation for her citizens' property in Czechoslovakia, which had been nationalized as a result of the party take-over—somewhere between forty and fifty million dollars. In return, we would ask that the embargo on the goods and materials we had already purchased be lifted, and, in addition, that we be permitted to borrow about one hundred million dollars to buy more materials in the United States.

As Dr. Outrata knew, we had already held some discussions with an American delegation and had been invited to continue these negotiations. It was extremely important, however, that I meet with Dean Acheson to explain the political background of the plan. I had had personal contact with Acheson before, and I hoped that, in talking with him, I could make him understand our approach to the problem of the cold war.

Our government attached great importance to these negotiations. We did not wish to follow Tito and break with the Soviet Union. She was our main ally, and we hoped to remain on the best of terms with her, both politically and economically. However, we did not want to break all ties with the West. In the political atmosphere created by Tito, we felt that our efforts to construct a friendly economic relationship with the West would have a tremendous impact, not only on our country but also on the relationship between East and West in general. As Czechoslovakia now had a key position in the Soviet bloc, this new type of foreign policy could make history.

Outrata listened carefully to all that I told him. But when I told him of my intention to meet with Mr. Acheson, who was then secretary of state of the United States of America, the Ambassador shook his head and told me that he felt such a meeting would be impossible to arrange.

I knew that in the United States, as in other countries, personal connections were more important than political ties or ideological affinities. Therefore, I had picked as a member of my delegation a former director general of a Czech bank who had been enjoying successful contacts with the United States for decades. That man knew a lawyer who was willing to forget that I and my country were Communist, for a one-percent commission. As the sum involved was forty million dollars, this was pretty handsome—

especially in those pre-inflation days. I told him that I had met Dean Acheson in Atlantic City several times with the former Foreign Minister of Czechoslovakia, Jan Masaryk, and he said he thought that Mr. Acheson might receive me once I had made my application through the usual diplomatic channels.

I do not know how the lawyer played it, but it is a fact that Acheson did receive me, and that he received me alone, without Ambassador Outrata. It was one more snub to the poor doctor, but he was so eager to score even the smallest success that he took it in the best of spirits.

The office into which I was ushered to meet Acheson was, to my surprise, very modest. It definitely did not look like the office of the secretary of state of the most prosperous and mighty country in the world. Perhaps Acheson met me in someone else's quarters, not wanting to make my visit too official.

In any case, when I was led into the small room in the State Department, Dean Acheson was already sitting behind the desk. He was extremely elegant, and, with his attractive mustache, looked more like an actor than a government official. He was very controlled in his behavior, very polite, and we sat a great distance from each other. I found him quick in the art of repartee and difficult to negotiate with, because he immediately sensed the weakness of any argument.

In speaking with Acheson, I realized that we were facing each other not only from opposite enemy trenches, so to speak, but also from different doctrines and prejudices. At that time, United States foreign policy was simply anti-Communist. Whether you were pink, red, or purple, whether Chinese, black, or white, once the label "Communist" was fixed on you, you were quickly and completely categorized. The fact that a Communist regime recently come to power and closely allied to the Soviet Union was trying to re-establish commercial ties with the United States made no impression on American policy makers. Even the heretic Tito was considered just another Communist; at that time, no effort was made to understand that, in spite of their similar revolutions and common Communist denominator, the various countries on the other side of the Iron Curtain had retained national traditions, individualities, and problems.

Nobody seemed to care that hundreds of millions of colonial people were being ruthlessly exploited by international (as well as American) companies; that the low prices of Cuban sugar, Costa Rican bananas, Arabian oil, Ghanaian cocoa, Brazilian coffee, and Chilean copper ensured that only starvation wages would be paid to the men and women who worked the fields and mines. And all this was happening at a time when the ancient structure of those countries had been seriously shaken by the events of World War II. It did not occur to anyone that peasants and workers in those countries were about as willing to put up with such conditions as the American subjects exploited by His Britannic Majesty King George had been, two hundred years earlier. The Americans, who freed themselves from foreign political and economic bondage, seemed to have forgotten their own Revolution and the help their ancestors had given to the French Revolution. Now they were supporting landowners, kings, aristocrats, sheiks—powers that stood for the past and would be swept away by the winds of history sooner or later.

Instead of recognizing the historical justice of national struggles for independence and recognition, American politicians branded all these national revolutions "Communist," as if whole peoples would sacrifice their lives because "Moscow whispered something in their ears."

It was this futile effort to stem the dynamic powers of history that forced many emerging countries into the Soviet Union's bear hug and actually helped the Communist parties radicalize the populations. Even where Communists were already in power, the situation was far from simple and monolithic.

I could not understand how professional politicians in the United States could be blind to the fact that economic relations with the various "satellites" would serve not only the Communist establishments of this or that country, but also the West, by providing the various governments with sufficient maneuvering room so that they would not be so completely dependent on Moscow.

Very carefully I tried to explain to this powerful man across the desk that, in spite of the vehemence of those who did not wish to cooperate with the United States, there were also strong forces in the party who hoped that such cooperation would be possible. This did not mean that Czechoslovakia would give up her close ties with the Soviet Union—we saw no reason why that should be necessary.

I told Acheson that our alliance and close friendship with the Soviet Union was the product of our bitter experience at Munich in 1938, when Czechoslovakia, who had a military alliance with France and a close friendship with Britain, was sold out to Hitler and Mussolini, not by her enemies, but by those who were pretending to be her friends.

Acheson replied to this by saying, "Well, if it is so, why didn't you accept the Marshall Plan? We offered you help, and you refused it."

I explained that Czechoslovakia had accepted the Marshall Plan, and that the government had changed its mind and rejected it only after Stalin intervened. We were told that accepting the Marshall Plan would be considered an inimical act against the Soviet Union and that it would have predictable political consequences. Not only the Czechoslovak Communist party, but also the middle-class, liberal parties then in the coalition government —this all happened before the party take-over—shrank from such a break. But now, securely in power, many leaders of the Czechoslovak Communist movement desired good relations with the U.S.A., as this would strengthen the economy and counterbalance an overly strong dependence on Moscow.

The interview lasted forty-five minutes, definitely longer than I expected. Acheson made no promises, but he thanked me for the interesting information and assured me that we would meet again.

And we did meet again. This time he informed me that the

embargo could not be lifted, but that the United States government would have no objections if we sold the goods to a third party.

Translated into plain commercial language, this meant that we would sell the embargoed material to a business contact in a neutral country and buy it back from them—albeit at a loss. With this end in mind, I began negotiations with the appropriate officials in the State Department, who were led by Mr. Hintze.

This was the procedure I discussed in my conversation with the Soviet commercial attaché with whom I met regularly during the course of my negotiations. I no longer recall his name; he was about my age, between forty and forty-five, and seemed to be extremely reserved, although, in retrospect, I realize that he was no more reserved than Dean Acheson. He offered me cigarettes, but no vodka, no tea, no coffee. He sat and listened, took notes, and asked a few questions, but he did not express any views of his own. It was obvious to me that he did not want to commit himself, but this was not particularly astonishing. I knew that Soviet officials never ventured their own political opinions until they got instructions from headquarters. In spite of this, I considered it my duty to inform him in depth, so that, through him, our Soviet friends would get the information from me and not from rumors.

It was said in Washington that the Soviet embassy did not need any locks, as the FBI was guarding the entrances so well that a mouse could not go in or out without their knowledge. I remember that once—only once—did the attaché come to the embassy after our Ambassador had invited him. He did not eat or drink, but just took notes, smoked, said thank you, and left.

Throughout the course of the negotiations I had also been reporting daily to Prague, but I never received an answer, comments, or new instructions; I was really not sure how President Gottwald would react to what I had done. In spite of that, I continued negotiations, convinced that we were serving not only my country, but also the interests of the great Socialist ideal I believed in.

I was not worried about disapproval from the Soviet Union. As long as I was acting in the best interests of Czechoslovak Socialism and on the orders of the Czechoslovak party leaders, I knew that I could not be in conflict with the Soviet Union.

My 1949 visit to Washington was very different from my previous trips, in 1943 and again in 1944, when I had come to negotiate with the UNRRA (United Nations Relief and Rehabilitation Administration) for the Czechoslovak government in exile. There was a war on at that time, and the Soviet Union was repelling the German troops with all her strength. Until Pearl Harbor, the United States had been strongly isolationist and rather conservative, contemptuous of the Soviet Union and of Socialism and its ideas and practices. But by 1943, the American people had become rather curious. They wanted to know who these Communists were, these strange animals with utopian ideas who suddenly were able to make such great exertions. And I was there at that time, a real live Communist, behaving quite normally, bridging East and West, and consuming beefsteaks with the best of them.

Everybody who knows Washington knows that nothing is secret there, and it soon became known that there was a Communist in the Czechoslovak government delegation who had been very successful in negotiating agreements with the leaders of the American administration in 1943 and 1944. One day, a gentleman came to my hotel and introduced himself as the representative of a consortium; he told me that his company wanted to set up an international import and export organization for all of Europe, with headquarters in Paris. He had come to offer me a top position in this organization, and I was to have a percentage of the turnover and a share in the profits.

I was naturally pleased to have earned such a reputation but felt that if I were to accept an offer outside of my government and my party, I would be selling myself for money and giving up the Socialist ideals for which I had lived.

I remember that, at the time, I felt not the slightest conflict; it just happened naturally. If my country and my government needed me, I would of course go where they sent me, and the issue of who paid me and how much was not important. I was deeply convinced that the only avenue for human society was that of Socialism. Hitler, Mussolini, and the Great Depression had taught me that capitalism was condemned to death and that if we wanted a humane world, without suffering, without war, without anti-Semitism and racial prejudice, the only way to achieve it was to begin with a Marxian base, under the leadership of a party that adhered to Marxism. This deep conviction was an integral part of me and the basis for all my values.

After the successful conclusion of my negotiations, Ambassador Outrata was overjoyed. He felt that my success was also his: the first success of Czechoslovak-American diplomacy since the party take-over in February of 1948.

Two days later, I got a telegram from the Minister of Foreign Affairs telling me that President Gottwald had awarded me the Gold Star of February, the highest order of the Czechoslovak Socialist Republic. Another telegram followed, with congratulations from the entire Communist party organization of my ministry. Dr. Outrata's wife organized a great Czechoslovakian dinner in my honor, complete with roast pork, dumplings and sauerkraut, and Pilsner beer.

Telegram after telegram was read, toast after toast drunk in my honor. I felt that nothing could happen to me, that I was on a boat destined to go from one success to another. Fate was with me.

Prague

Flying from New York to Prague in 1949 was quite an experience. The trip took over thirty hours, with stops in Reykjavík in Iceland, Shannon in Ireland, and finally in London.

Czechoslovakia is a tiny country—a mere fifty thousand square miles with fewer than fifteen million Czechs and Slovaks living on it. But whenever I returned home from abroad, I marveled at the miracle of how so many beautiful features could be compressed into such a small territory. High and low mountains, valleys and flatlands, villages, lonely farms, and one of the most beautiful cities in the world—a mixture of old traditions and modern spirit, rich in culture. There was Romanesque and medieval art, a highly advanced theater, cinema, and painting. The country was permeated with music; in a city of a million like Prague, there were four philharmonic orchestras, and two opera houses. It was the poet Nezval who said that culture was the religion of the Czech and Slovak peoples. No wonder, for it was their culture that helped them to survive three hundred years of German and Hungarian domination.

And now—and now we ordained that we should build a new type of Socialism in this country with an old tradition, a democratic culture, and an industrious population. Our country had not been destroyed by war; our factories were intact and would now—so I dreamed—be harnessed to the interests of the Czechoslovak and world proletariat.

When the plane touched down in Prague, I was so happy to be

home again that I forgot to collect my papers and lock my diplomatic pouch before we landed. I remember putting on my coat in a completely empty plane. I was the last one left on board.

As I stood at the top of the exit stairs looking into the spring sunshine, I felt fulfilled. Compared with the big airports in America and in Britain, these ramshackle buildings in Prague were terribly poor, but I did not see things that way then. Like all of us, I saw a future superimposed on the gray present, a Socialist Czechoslovakia of which I had the luck to be one of the chief architects.

A crowd of reporters were waiting for me in the airport lobby—representatives from our party newspaper, *Rudé Pravo* (Red Right), and all the other papers, and also some journalists from the fraternal Socialist countries. The few correspondents from the West who had remained in Prague after the party took over were asking me questions even before I stepped to the ground.

They wanted to know about the negotiations, what had been accomplished in Washington, when the talks would resume, whether an announcement on some final agreement would come soon. I told them that the negotiations were going well and that I expected to return to Washington sometime during the winter.

I was working my way through the crowd when a man in a black raincoat and a black hat appeared at my side.

"The President is waiting for you at the Hradcin palace, Mr. Deputy Minister."

He cleared a path through the crowd and guided me across the airport lobby to a side entrance where another man was waiting next to a long black limousine with white tires. It was a Russian ZIS—a remake of the Ford, built by the Soviets in Gorki—and it was Stalin's personal gift to President Gottwald. I felt it was a great honor to ride in the President's own car, an honor that is not bestowed often or freely, and, more than this, a sign that the President had approved my suggestions, that my position had been solidified.

I was happy, excited, and about to explode with pride. My suggestions for foreign trade policy had been accepted. I had made it. The whole ministry would be running along the lines I indicated.

I lit my pipe and looked through the window at the outskirts of Prague speeding by. It was a little childish, perhaps, but I remember distinctly that I thought of my mother. I suddenly saw her in front of me—I almost felt her there—and I said something like, "Mother, you should be here to see this."

I did not think about my mother very often. She died of diabetes in 1917. Before the discovery of insulin, the diagnosis of diabetes was equivalent to a death sentence. I was ten years old when she died, and I was present at her deathbed. Although I could barely remember what she looked like, I felt her absence all my life, and whenever something important happened to me, I wished that she could be there with me.

During World War I, when my father was in the army, she had to run the family business. In the mornings, while she combed her hair, we would talk about the war, about the soldiers home on leave, and I tried to convince her that if I were in command of the army, we would already have won. She listened to me with a tolerant smile, but took my strategic plans as seriously as I did.

"When the time comes," she used to say, "you'll do something even more important than win wars."

And now, Mother, I thought as we rode through Prague, I have done something more important, something much more important.

I was forty-two years old. Without the Communist party I would never have become a deputy minister, or even a government official. Actually, I had had no large ambitions to start with. I had been an employee in an insurance company and might have stayed there all my life. I became a member of the party because of an inner need, a commitment to the cause of the workers.

In retrospect, I can see that my idealism was not wholly pure; there was the temptation of, perhaps, suddenly becoming one of the main movers and actors on the stage of history—all the more seductive since one feels one is acting for what is good while combining it with a personal career. One's actions are supported by an ideology.

When the President's car entered the first courtyard of the ancient castle and rolled past the cathedral of St. Guy to the majestic royal wing, I saw the soldiers presenting arms. To me. I felt as if I were riding on clouds. Inside, there was a huge old marble staircase with the white carpet and the golden chandeliers.

At the bottom of these stairs, a civilian was waiting for me. "Comrade Loebl?"

Just like that. Any other citizen would have had to show his identity card, that internal passport which had been introduced quite recently to control everyone's movements. But not I! Not even my party card. Nothing. I walked up—no, I floated up those stairs, turned to the right, and was led into the private apartment of the President.

I believe that President Gottwald understood that his living in the castle of the Czech kings had a symbolic meaning. He saw in himself a representative of the working class, a member of its elite and vanguard, the Communist party. Originally a turner, Gottwald had worked within the party until 1929 when, at the height of the Depression, he gathered sufficient support and took over the party.

Gottwald was married to a former waitress named Marta with whom he had had an illegitimate daughter. They met in Slovakia in the late twenties, while she was working in a small tavern. When Gottwald became prime minister, and later president, Marta grew terribly fat and tried to play first lady. While he moved with natural ease among the splendors of the castle, his wife ordered dresses from the most expensive middle-class fashion houses and wore them on the most inappropriate occasions. There were countless anecdotes about her—how she scratched her hair with a fork, how she mixed up "conservation" with "conversation," and many others.

Gottwald was a squat man with a ruddy face and a bulbous

nose. A politician all his life, he had great self-confidence; now, crowned with success, he could afford to be very pleasant. He had an earthy sense of humor, he sucked on his pipe when he was not smoking it, and he accepted criticism extremely well. One day, while talking to him, I even said, "This is nonsense" several times, but he was not offended.

He behaved like a man who owns a farm and is interested in its management. Indeed, he acted as if he owned the Republic and showed a great interest in all details. He was a dictator and had dictatorial powers, but he used them in a very paternalistic way when dealing with his collaborators.

He was far from erudite, but he had a fantastic memory. He remembered everything that caught his interest, even phrases and formulations I had uttered and since forgotten. Also, he had extraordinary common sense, a Czech type of common sense, down to earth, realistic, and not carried away with wishful thinking.

He always insisted that things be explained to him in a straightforward way, and I had to organize my material and information accordingly whenever I was to meet with him. I confess that I liked Gottwald very much and even used to call him by his nickname, "Klema," until he became president. At that time I was informed that the Politburo had decided that we should not call him "Klema" any more, but "Comrade President," and from then on I called him that.

Gottwald was ill. I was told that his blood circulation was very poor, and he had to take a pill every hour or so. He also limped a little on his right leg, but at the time of my visit, I was not paying attention to his limp.

When I entered his apartment, he motioned me to come nearer, shook my hand, embraced me, and congratulated me on my reports, my negotiations, and my success. He then opened a drawer in his desk and took out a small black leather case. Handing it to me, he told me that he was proud to award me the party's highest honor, the Gold Star of February, for the conclusion of my negotiations in the United States and Great Britain.

Since the President knew the details of the negotiations from my dispatches, my report to him at this time was merely a summary. He was amused at the Washington lawyer who arranged a meeting with a political personality for a bribe (he would not accept the word "commission"); he found it quite natural that in a capitalist country you could buy everything and everybody, and this incident just confirmed his beliefs.

The chances for improving trade with the United States were good, and I reported to Gottwald on the various corporations through which I had arranged to promote the sales of Czechoslovak glass, china, costume jewelry, artificial flowers, and textile goods all over the United States. The city of New Orleans had awarded me honorary citizenship to prove its interest and wanted to be our port of entry into the U.S. There were many groups of Americans interested in Czech imports, especially Jewish importers who appreciated our aid to Israel.

In those days, Czechoslovakia and other countries of the Soviet bloc were supplying the young Israeli army not only with small arms, but also with tanks and guns; Israeli recruits were training in Czechoslovak army camps. When the Egyptians offered us gold for the excellent arms of the Brno and Strakonice small-arms factories, Andrei Vishinsky himself, returning from a United Nations session in New York City (he was the Soviet delegate at the time), met with me and Clementis at Prague airport during a stopover and gave us strict instructions to reserve our supplies only for Israel.

I also told President Gottwald that I had, naturally, kept the Soviet embassy informed of all my negotiations in Washington. He found that quite normal and said that he would stress it to Moscow.

Finally, he told me that I should inform the Economic Council in person of my visit to America and that I should mention that he agreed, in principle, with everything I had done there; trade with the United States was on the agenda of the next Politburo meeting, and he planned to discuss it at that time.

I left his office in time to be home for dinner. I had called my wife from the airport to say that I had to see the President and would not be home until later. Now she and my son were waiting.

My wife, Fritzi, was not a Communist, but she was very sympathetic to the aims of the party and the establishment of the just Socialist world order of which I was dreaming. I think that my firmly held beliefs and dreams were one of the reasons she had married me. My work had separated the two of us before. When the party leadership sent me to Poland in 1938, after the Nazi occupation, she was forced to stay behind in Czechoslovakia. Later she left for Italy, and we were reunited in London only after a long and very strenuous year. It was always good to be home and with her once more.

The only present I brought her from America was a pair of nylon stockings—something that all women in Czechoslovakia were yearning for. The present for my son, Ivan, was equally modest—a fountain pen and a pullover—but at that time we all were modest. Our salaries were so small that even ordinary coffee and tea were great luxuries.

Fritzi and Ivan shared my feeling of happiness. When I opened the leather box in front of their eyes, the Gold Star of February sparkled in the light of our chandelier.

We were talking about my triumph when suddenly the bell to the apartment rang. I went to the door to find the President's secretary standing there.

"The President wants you. He sent me here to accompany you back."

I was surprised and more than a little puzzled. I had left the President less than two hours before: what could he want?

Gottwald was sitting on a sofa in the small baroque living room, and his face was flushed. He was not alone. Sitting across from him was the gray eminence of Czechoslovak politics, Comrade Bedrich Geminder.

"I'm sorry to disturb your homecoming, but Geminder, here, has just returned from Moscow. He had some interesting discussions with the Soviet party comrades, and one of the things they talked about was your mission to the United States."

Geminder nodded. He was a man of small stature, rather shy, and a very bad speaker. Coming from a part of Czechoslovakia where German and Polish were spoken in addition to Czech, he had not mastered any of these languages. His Czech was awful, his German incorrect; his Polish and Russian had a very strong accent.

I met Geminder for the first time in 1947, when Gottwald—at that time prime minister—invited me to speak about the Five-Year Plan at a dinner. Geminder was then on intimate terms with Gottwald and his wife. The President's wife knew him from Moscow, where they had lived in the same hotel. She called him by a diminutive of his first name, "Bedya," and treated him more as an older sister or a mother would treat a child.

I have forgotten exactly what Geminder said, but it went something like this: the Soviet party leadership saw the USSR as the bulwark of Socialism, and the Communist party of the Soviet Union as the vanguard of the working-class parties of the world. A threat to the Soviet Union and the Communist party of the Soviet Union would naturally be a mortal threat to the cause of Socialism everywhere. It was in the interest of all countries to strengthen the Soviet Union and the party of the Bolsheviks.

Then, too, the United States and Great Britain represented the unholy alliance of world imperialism in the eyes of the Soviet leadership. They could not see how there could be cooperation with imperialist countries in view of this deadly threat.

That was where Tito had made his mistake. His error—said Geminder—was to believe that the United States would be willing to cooperate with a Socialist country. In reality, the U.S.A. wanted merely to split the Socialist bloc, destroy its unity, and swallow its components piecemeal.

Why should Czechoslovakia, of all countries, encourage such a tactic? Would it not be better to lose the forty million dollars the United States held embargoed and show the world and all the Socialist countries what criminals the Americans really were?

And anyway, Czechoslovakia did not need capitalist technology, as it had Soviet Socialist technology at its disposal.

At that time, the victorious Red Army of Chairman Mao, Chou En-lai, and Chu Teh was resting on its laurels, having driven Generalissimo Chiang Kai-shek to Taiwan. With 750 million Chinese as their allies, the Soviet leadership saw one third of humanity under their control. The Socialist bloc seemed to them invincible, and they felt that it would be only a matter of time until the capitalist countries would collapse.

I saw the President getting up from his sofa and limping across the room. He seemed much tenser than when I had seen him in the afternoon. Geminder continued:

"Loebl should write articles, speak on the radio, perhaps hold a press conference and talk about his experiences in the United States. He should emphasize that the American embargo is a hostile act directed against all Socialist countries and that it is designed to bring starvation and misery to people simply because they do not support capitalism."

Suddenly the President shouted, "Our people are not Russian *muzhik*s!" He walked over to where Geminder was sitting and glared at him. I realized that Gottwald was drunk. He continued: "We will do nothing of the kind. I have no intention of having Loebl say that nonsense to anyone. He and you and all of us will say nothing. We are the friends and allies of the Soviet Union and will remain friends and allies of the Soviet Union, but we have our own problems and we will solve them in our own way. During the war, Stalin said that we would have to find a Czechoslovak way to Socialism, and that's exactly what I intend to do. I gave in to Stalin when he wanted us to get out of the Marshall Plan, but I won't give in again."

He stopped, and apparatchik Geminder hurried to respond. Only now he sounded more like Gottwald than Gottwald himself. The party line had changed, and Geminder, the perfect party man, changed with it.

We talked a while longer, and it was agreed that we would keep trying to come to some kind of détente with the West without giving any special justification to Moscow for doing it. Nor would we answer the Soviet theoretical criticism, except to assure them that we were their very good friends.

It was almost midnight. After an eight-hour flight from Moscow, Geminder was dead tired and asked to be excused. I was also tired. I said good-by to the President and started for the door.

"Wait a minute, I'd like you to stay."

I went back into the drawing room and sat on the sofa next to Gottwald. He got up and started limping back and forth across the room, smoking his pipe.

There was a coffee table with a bottle of red wine on it, and every time he passed it, the President took a sip. When he finished one bottle, his butler brought another. It was well known that Gottwald was a drinker, even though the doctor had warned him that drinking would aggravate his heart condition. But this was the first time I saw him drunk, and I was surprised at the change that came over him.

He said that Stalin was disagreeing with his policy; otherwise the man from the Soviet Central Committee would never have contacted Geminder. But if Stalin didn't like what Gottwald was doing, why didn't he tell him so himself? Why did he have some departmental head send Geminder to do it for him? Didn't he realize that Gottwald was a head of state just as Stalin was?

He put down his glass and continued. He knew very well what he owed to Stalin, and he was grateful to him. Without Stalin's help, he would never have become president. But didn't Stalin realize that Czechoslovakia was an independent country, and that he, Gottwald, would do what was best for Czechoslovakia?

He stopped, quite close to me, and I saw tiny beads of sweat on his red face.

"Stalin, that son of a bitch"—he actually did say "that son of a bitch"—"who does he think he is, that he can treat me like his messenger boy? I am a worker—and who is he? He studied theology. *Theology.* I devoted my whole life to the workers' movement and to the Soviet Union. I am the first worker-president of Czechoslovakia. I will do what is best for the working class. I was the one who made up the slogan 'With the Soviet Union forever.' *With* the Soviet Union. The *two* of us. Czechoslovakia *and* the Soviet Union, partners. Together."

He took another sip. Poured another glass.

"You did a good job, Jantchi. We will stay on the same road. I'm not going to be another Tito or another Rakossi."

At that time, Tito's name was never mentioned publicly without epithets like "bloody pig" or "lackey of the imperialists" or "spittle-licker of capitalism," while the Hungarian Communist party boss, Matyas Rakossi, an absolute Stalinist, was an obedient puppet of the Soviet administration.

I was surprised to hear Gottwald call me "Jantchi," the nickname only my closest friends used. Gottwald was a friendly boss, but he had always kept his distance.

I saw him walking away from me across the room. Suddenly he turned and shouted: "I am Klement Gottwald. Klement Gottwald! And Czechoslovakia will be *Gottwald's* Czechoslovakia, not Stalin's."

He stopped at the table and took another sip of wine.

"Listen, Jantchi, you like to make theories, to argue about things with ideology. Forget it. Don't talk about what you're doing, just do it. Always talk friendship with the Soviet Union, but *do* what is good for us."

Then he started to repeat himself, to say whole sentences over and over. He began slurring his words, and it became very difficult to understand him. Finally, he sat down in an armchair and fell asleep. Around three o'clock, his butler came in to take him to bed, and I asked him to call a guard to take me home.

I went home in the President's car, and all around me was the sleeping city. A few trucks rumbled by, but there was no one in the streets. At that time, we lived in two floors of an old house in a beautiful part of Prague. The apartment had three bedrooms, a study, a large living room, a dining room, and a balcony off the living room that overlooked a small garden. In short, it was one of those apartments that are strictly reserved for the governing elite in a Socialist country, for those few who run the country and live a pampered life. And I was part of this ruling elite.

The relatively low salaries of people in high government positions were aimed at giving the impression of equality of income. If one considered the salaries alone, such an assumption appeared correct. But there were remarkable "fringe benefits" that made the power elite also an economic elite. We, for instance, had our beautiful apartment virtually rent free, and I had a car and a driver at my disposal. All the parties I gave were catered by a special firm and charged to the ministry. I had special medical privileges and could at any time make use of spas or recreation centers of my choice; I could travel freely and enjoyed hundreds of small privileges that were not available to ordinary citizens—and particularly not to the "ruling" proletariat.

We took these privileges for granted, as a reward given by the party leadership—the highest moral, political, and economic authority. These privileges also had a deep psychological impact: they made us more willing to serve the party in order to merit the rewards, and we became increasingly desensitized toward those who did not share in them. Such people probably did not deserve them!

When I came in, my wife and son were sleeping. Being far too excited to sleep, I made myself some coffee and went out to sit on the balcony. A few birds were chirping in the darkness, but otherwise the night was absolutely still. Sitting in my easy chair and smoking, sipping strong black coffee, I tried to make some sense out of what Gottwald had said.

I had been an economist all my life. Even now, as deputy minister of foreign trade, I was concerned chiefly with commercial and economic problems. This was the first time I realized that what I was doing had tremendous *political* implications. I still did not grasp how great the implications would be for my own life.

As the sun came up, I dozed off. It was morning when Fritzi found me asleep in my armchair.

After my return from the United States, I suddenly found

myself very popular. I was not officially promoted, but in the weeks that followed I was a frequent guest of leading members of the government—the Politburo, the President—and I was besieged with requests for appointments by ambassadors from the West.

I was suddenly surrounded with so much attention and good will that it practically overwhelmed me. When I made a joke, even if it was a trite one, people laughed. When I said a kind word to someone, he appeared deeply moved because it was a kind word from me.

I was flattered, but I missed confrontation with other people; I like arguments, and I was not having any. Everyone just wanted to find out what I thought so that they could agree with it.

I started to feel isolated. I had so many new friends that my old friends, my real friends, did not want to share their company. They were afraid I might think that they were attracted to me just because I was *en vogue*.

The Central Committee

Power has its rewards, and it brought me a feeling of freedom and self-fulfillment. A powerful man can do as he pleases, and people around him will adapt to whatever he does. My power and popularity were the obvious proof of what I had believed all along: that honestly following my own ideas was the real key to success. Without having tried to be a conformist, a line-toer, I found myself hailed as a great man, a man who was as successful at opening up trade with the West as he had been two years earlier in making agreements with the Soviets, the Poles, the Yugoslavs, and the Bulgars. I felt as if I were the architect of my small country's life. Of her foreign trade. Securing for her essential raw materials, the lifeblood of her industry.

I saw nothing special one day early in September of 1949 when I was summoned to the office of the chief of personnel of the Central Committee of the party—the head of the so-called Cadre Department. I would meet him in the course of my duties every two weeks or so; in a Communist country, no one can be in a leading position without consulting this department. One could call it the personnel department of the party, for it decides which person should occupy this or that job. The Cadre Department operates on the local level, the county level, and even a level as high as a ministry of the party Central Committee.

If I wanted to appoint a commercial attaché or a commercial counselor in an embassy, I needed the approval of the Cadre Department. On the other hand, if they wanted to promote someone the party was particularly interested in, they would ask if I had any objections.

The driver of the ministry car dropped me in front of the party headquarters building and pulled the black limousine up in the parking space reserved for the cars of visiting VIPs. At that time, the Central Committee was occupying a large building, formerly a bank, in the center of town. Built in the mid-thirties by one of the most progressive of Czechoslovakia's architects, it stood six stories high and the equivalent of three stories deep, gleaming white, boxlike beside the fifteenth-century Gothic powder tower.

There was a white marble staircase leading up to the rooms that had been occupied by the chairman of the board and the managers of the once-mighty bank. Now behind the leather-covered doors dwelt the General Secretary of the party, Rudolf Slansky, his gray eminence, Bedrich Geminder, and the head of party security, Karel Svab.

As I walked up the steps, I thought this was going to be a routine discussion, and I expected to talk about other people's problems—not my own. I remember passing the security check on the first floor, being checked again in the elevator, and finally being ushered into the office of Ladislav Kopriva, the head of the Cadre Department.

Kopriva was in his late forties or early fifties. He was always very well dressed, and on his lapel he wore a party insignia, the red star with the hammer and sickle and the Czechoslovakian flag. I wore it, too.

When I entered his office, he was very formal and polite. I was still the deputy minister of foreign trade and deserved respect. After a few minutes of small talk, he dialed the phone and said to whoever answered, "Comrade Loebl is here."

While we were waiting, he asked me how business was and if there were any problems. I filled my pipe and he gave me a light, and we had a friendly discussion. Then the door opened and Karel Svab, head of party security, entered.

Among other things, Svab was responsible for the police and

law enforcement. He was the brother of the Politburo member Mrs. Svermova, the dowager widow of Jan Sverma, a Communist leader and national hero who died mysteriously during the abortive Slovak uprising in 1944.

Svab was an old party member, a prewar party member. During the war, he had been in a German concentration camp. I did not know him well, but we had met two or three times at receptions. He was considered a very powerful and reliable man and was trusted by both the Soviet and the Czech Politburos. Small, thin, and somewhat handsome, he had a strange, uninflected way of speaking, rattling through each sentence as if there were no punctuation. He gave the impression of being a very strict, orthodox man, absolutely correct, unapproachable, and not to be bribed. And yet he was the only man who would actually hit me.

Svab greeted me with the special party greeting, *"Cest praci"* ("Your work be honored"). We shook hands, and he went immediately to the business at hand. He spoke at length about Anglo-American imperialism which tried to destroy Socialism, about the danger of imperialist encroachment, about the cold war that was getting colder. He spoke of enemies who tried to infiltrate the party; after all, I knew what had happened in Hungary, where a member of the ruling Politburo, one of the most trusted Communists, had actually confessed to having been an informer for the Nazi Gestapo and a spy for the U.S. Central Intelligence Agency. After Tito's attempt to split the world Socialist movement, Svab said, it ought to be understood that each party member must be vigilant and must immediately disclose to the proper authorities everything he knew. Sometimes people didn't realize with whom they were talking. Too trusting and naïve, such people could do the greatest harm.

From what he said, I got the impression that I would be asked to help the party in its attempts to foil those Anglo-American spies, but he made two or three allusions that made me feel that there was more to it. I remember his telling me, "You realize,

Comrade Loebl, that everything depends on how frank you will be."

As he said this for the second and third time, it became clear to me that something else was at stake besides general information. I said that of course I was prepared to be absolutely frank, that I was ready to answer any questions he might ask, and that he would get a completely truthful answer. I was told that this was not just a matter of questions and answers.

He said that he wanted me to type my entire life story and that this autobiography should be very, very frank. And I should realize that everything depended on how frank I would be in this biography of mine. It should be a sort of "deposition."

At first I was surprised, and then stunned, as if I had been hit and could not feel the pain right away. As he led me out of the office and into an elevator to one of the upper floors of the building, I realized what he had not said: that I was under suspicion, possibly even under arrest, that there must have been a denunciation, naturally unjust—because I was absolutely convinced that I had done nothing that could be disapproved of.

I remember how hurt I felt that despite my devotion and my desire to do the best for the party and for the country, somebody could suspect me.

As I followed him through the angular corridor built in the German *Neue Sachlichkeit* style, the sound of our footsteps reverberated as in a cathedral. By chance, he brought me to the office of the National Economic Commission, the very office where I had worked out the Five-Year Plan. He opened the door, ushered me in, and said that someone would bring a typewriter. And he repeated that I should be honest and frank, that I should write down everything, no matter how trite it might seem, and that everything depended on how well I carried out this task. With that, he walked out and closed the door behind him.

I did not know what to think. Less than an hour before, I had left my office as practically the head of a ministry, popular and respected, with every chance of an even greater career ahead of me. Now I was sitting in an office at the party headquarters, assigned to report every conversation and contact I had ever had, privately as well as publicly, and prove, if I could, that I was not a traitor.

Then the door opened and in came a guard, carrying a typewriter, and Mrs. Jarmila Taussig, an employee of the Control Commission. Mrs. Taussig was a middle-aged lady of middle-class origins who embraced the doctrine of the world proletariat with religious fervor. No personal relationships, no family ties, no love was more important to her than the party. Four years later, I was to share a cell with a man named Honza Cernik, an old party member, who told me that he had worked with Mrs. Taussig in the party youth movement and that they had lived together for a while. They had met while distributing illegal pamphlets together, and the second time he saw her, he asked her to come to his apartment. At first she hesitated, then let him kiss her. Suddenly she pulled away and said, "Honza, do you really love Comrade Stalin?"

He readily confessed that he very much adored Comrade Stalin, and so nothing stood in the way of their bliss. . . . In those days, there were many young men who loved Comrade Stalin.

The party oligarchy was so small that everybody knew everybody else, but in front of the guard, Mrs. Taussig behaved as if I were a stranger. She pointed out that this was the typewriter I should use and there was the paper, that I would be served lunch, and that I was not supposed to leave the room or use the telephone.

I paced up and down, wondering what to do. Maybe I should not write anything. Or just write that everything I had done, I had done in the interest of the party, and that I did not feel it was necessary to defend myself.

And then I thought that that might be the wrong thing to do. There had been a general nervousness in the party for weeks, starting late in the summer with the trial of Laszlo Rajk. Rajk was a Hungarian Communist who had devoted his entire life to the party and its cause. He was born into a well-to-do Jewish family in Budapest. Hungary was then an old-fashioned feudal dictatorship run by the land-owning aristocracy and the middle class. The government was led by an ancient admiral named Miklós Horthy, a ruthless man who was closely affiliated with Mussolini.

After helping to organize an underground Communist party in Hungary, Rajk volunteered to take part in the Spanish Civil War. He served in the international brigades that fought on the Loyalist side against Franco.

When, in the fall of 1938, the Loyalists were defeated and had to flee across the snow-covered Pyrenees, Rajk surrendered to the French police. The French government interned all refugees from Spain in a notorious concentration camp in Gurs.

Two years later, after the fall of France, the prisoners were handed over to the Gestapo, and Rajk's incarceration continued in a German concentration camp. He survived there, thanks to the Communist prisoners who had organized to assist one another, and returned to Soviet-occupied Hungary after the war.

In 1948 Rajk became a member of the fourteen-man governing committee, the Politburo, a member of the strategic party Secretariat, and, finally, minister of the interior. (In the latter capacity, he was responsible for the imprisonment of Hungary's Cardinal Mindszenty.) Post after post and honor after honor were heaped upon him, and, in May 1949, he seemed to be the most highly acclaimed party leader.

But only a month later, on June 16, Rajk was arrested, accused of being a fascist spy, a Trotskyite, and, worst of all, an ally and accomplice of the Yugoslav renegade, Tito.

During their show trial, which took place in September of 1949, Laszlo Rajk and his companions were accused not only of complicity with Tito, but also of spying and of having conspiratorial connections with two Americans—the brothers Herman and Noel Field. Through them, Rajk and his associates were supposed to have been connected with Allen Dulles and his Central Intelligence Agency.

At the end of the trial, which was widely reported in the Czech press, Rajk actually did confess that while he was in Spain he had become an agent of the Hungarian fascist secret police, that he was an agent of Tito, and that he was also spying for the Americans. And as his confession was so complete, he was duly hanged.

Strange as it may seem today, Rajk's instructive biography did not impress itself on our consciousness at the time. Possibly we did not want to think about that strange trial, just as people do not take notice of death unless it happens close to them.

Only a few days after Rajk's conviction, Ludvik Frejka, one of Gottwald's closest aides, told me that the trial had had an anti-Czechoslovak aspect, and that the Soviets were preparing something against us. It was clear to me that he was repeating the views of Gottwald and the party leadership, and I knew what he was referring to.

One of the defendants confessed that he was part of a Titoist group whose leaders were members of the Czech party. He also confessed that that group intended to lead Czechoslovakia and the rest of the Socialist countries in Eastern Europe out of the Socialist camp and into an alliance with the West. All over Prague, people started to wonder who might be part of that possible conspiracy. Everyone began to suspect everyone else. People who had had the luck to be permitted to spend a summer in Yugoslavia were suddenly regretting they ever had that holiday at the Adriatic coast and felt that they were under suspicion.

A good deal of informing and backbiting had gone on all over Europe, when people liberated from the Nazi yoke denounced their personal enemies as German collaborators. Now the same was happening in Prague. Frequently, personal differences were at the bottom of the suspicions voiced against so-called conspirators. I knew of many such cases in the Ministry of Foreign Trade; but as this mutual back-stabbing went on mostly in the higher ranks of the party, I assumed that I was suspected because someone had used the commercial treaty I made with the Yugoslavs in 1947, and my strong support of trade with Yugoslavia, as proof of treason.

It seemed to me, then, that I was being accused on trumped-up charges, and that all I needed to do was to write the truth and rebut these patently false accusations. The more I thought about my position, the more I felt that it was my duty to tell the truth, and to do everything I could to help the truth be discovered and established.

And I also realized that Comrade Svab's admonishment was quite to the point: I should be extremely careful not to forget anything, because the things I omitted might be as dangerous to me as the things I wrote about. Leaving out some person or some event might be regarded as an attempt to cover up the individuals involved.

But my conscience was clear. I could write about everything and everybody; I had nothing to hide. So in order not to give the impression that I did have something to hide, I concentrated on remembering all the people of importance I had met and talked to, particularly in America and Great Britain during and after the war and during my negotiations in Yugoslavia, France, and other European countries.

I typed more than a hundred pages, working a good sixteen hours a day for two days. I was in a very strange psychological state—in limbo, suspended between heaven and hell.

My prevailing thought was that since I was absolutely innocent, nothing could happen to me. Besides, everything I had done had been done with the consent, and sometimes at the explicit orders, of the highest authorities in the party.

I assumed that in the ranks of the party there were indeed enemies of Socialism who wanted to compromise people currently in leading positions. I knew that one of the defendants in Budapest had said that the center of the anti-Soviet activities was in Czechoslovakia, and I considered it quite possible that some-one—maybe someone high up—might try to throw a spoke in the wheel. In fact, a saboteur might easily want to undermine the position of a man like me, someone who was doing his best for Socialism and his country.

Sitting alone in the emptiness of that big office, I found such an intrigue quite plausible. But I stuck to the more pleasant thought that it was all a mistake and would be cleared up eventually.

When it got dark outside the first night, they took me to another room on that floor, where a bed and a night table had been set up. I was told not to switch off the light; if I needed to use the bathroom, I was to knock on the door, and the guard would escort me down the hall. I slept very badly, tossing and turning late into the night, eager to get on with my writing. At daybreak, I sat down again at my typewriter. Whenever I finished two or three pages, someone came in and took them away.

Very late that night, Mrs. Taussig returned to the office where I was typing to tell me that I could go home. With her was a man named Bedrich Doubek who was to play a great part in my trial.

He was thin, about forty, polite, and, by his looks, obviously of the "worker cadre." He was one of those workers who, just because of their class origin, were selected for positions of trust —in the party and in all aspects of social life.

Doubek told me that what I had written would be carefully scrutinized, and he thanked me for giving such detailed information. There was only one other question he wanted to ask, and that was, why hadn't I explained why I joined the Communist party? After all, I had been born into a middle-class family and was a well-off intellectual. For a worker like him, it was natural to join the party of the working class, but it was very different for a member of the class that was the enemy of the proletariat.

This question made me furious. I had been a loyal member of the party for fifteen years. I joined in the thirties, when Hitler and Mussolini were rising to power, when my association with the Communist party could have meant only persecution. I had given them all the necessary information, but to answer a question like that was beneath my dignity.

My three interrogators were shocked at this response. They looked at one another and did not know what to say. My outburst was totally unexpected. After a pause, Mrs. Taussig forced a smile and said that I had answered the question with sufficient clarity; they would include the answer in their report. However, I was instructed not to mention to anyone where I had been. Doing so would be considered revealing a state secret and would land me in jail.

I was ordered to hand over my passport, since I would no longer be permitted to leave the country. As if this was not enough, I was also instructed to report to Mrs. Taussig by phone every day, including Sundays. Should I leave Prague, I would have to report to the security officer of the party in whatever city I traveled to.

I remember that when I returned home it was past midnight. I let myself in with the latchkey and tiptoed into the bedroom. Fritzi was already sleeping, and I did not wake her up. In the morning, she was very relieved to see me. I had told her two days before that I might not come home for a while, as I would be at a conference outside of Prague, but she had been very worried; there were many rumors at that time. I told her not to tell anyone about the conference, and I think she believed that that was where I had been. Then I went back to work.

The Ministry of Foreign Trade was also in a bank, an exquisite private bank which used to belong to a rich Jewish family, the Petscheks, before the war. The Petscheks had owned mostly mining, chemical, and textile interests in prewar Czechoslovakia, and, with their flair for international finance, they had sold out their Czechoslovakian holdings a year before Hitler destroyed the Republic.

When the Germans occupied Prague in 1939, they took over the bank and made it the headquarters of their dreaded secret police, the Gestapo. In the basement, there was a huge, empty room called "the cinema," because prisoners of the Nazis were forced to sit motionless staring at the blank wall as if it were a screen. In the cellars, in vaults that used to hold gold and securities, countless prisoners of the Gestapo were beaten to death or shot in the nape of the neck.

After my return, nobody was told about what had happened to me, but somehow it was in the air. People in the ministry continued to address me as First Deputy Minister, and I was still directing foreign trade, giving instructions to the commercial attachés at embassies all over the world; but now I was not allowed to leave Prague for a weekend without first getting permission.

I attended cabinet meetings, gave interviews, spoke on the radio, and negotiated with ambassadors, just as if nothing had happened. But somehow everything was changed. People seemed to know that I had been at party headquarters for questioning. They had no way of knowing what had happened there, and yet I felt that they were wondering what would become of me, whether I would remain a person of influence or simply disappear.

It so happened that I had planned a dinner party for a number of friends two nights after the interrogation. Now, one by one, they or their wives called to tell me how terribly sorry they were that they would not be able to come. Each one said how unhappy he was that something had come up and that he would be looking forward to seeing me, his dear friend, some time soon.

Everyone I met was exceedingly polite, but it was a very strange politeness. People did not know what was going to happen to me, so they were not sure they should risk being friendly to me. They all acted ambiguously, in such a way that they would be prepared whether I was given an advancement, the sack, or something worse. Many of the people I considered my best friends adopted this restricted kind of friendship, though others, whom I hardly knew, were ostentatiously friendly.

I was not offended, just somewhat saddened. I understood this behavior. In the growing polarization of our society, people were choosing their official contacts and even their friendships very carefully. Association with someone who was suspect might have serious repercussions for a man in a leading position. We were all exercising such caution; I probably chose my friends and reacted to invitations the same way.

No one knew what I was being charged with, including me. Something was happening that would either help me or hurt me, but no one seemed to know where or why, or who was going to decide. It occurred to me that maybe even the ones who were going to make the decision were waiting for some word, some explanation, some directive from above. In the meantime, nothing was what it seemed to be, no one said what they really thought—again, including me.

The day after my interrogation, I left my apartment early in the morning so I could clear up the work I had missed at the ministry. The streets were still empty, but as I passed a side street, I saw two men in a car at the corner. Looking in my rearview mirror, I saw that they were following me to the ministry.

From that day onward, I was followed wherever I went, whether to the theater, to a movie house, or even to the office of the Prime Minister or the President. I felt that everyone around me would notice that I was being followed, and this made me very nervous. But no one did, not even my wife. I remember we went to the cinema together; I noticed a man following us, but she did not.

I thought of challenging my followers, but I changed my mind. I guessed that they would reply that they were just doing their job. And, after all, it *was* their job. If I made too much of a fuss, those who were in charge would take it as a sign of bad conscience.

True, their boss, the Minister of the Interior, Vaclav Nosek, was a very good friend of mine. We had known each other since the war, when, as members of the party cell, we were both exiled in London. But being a deputy minister myself, I realized that possibly Nosek would not even have been notified of such a surveillance if it was only routine. If he had been notified, and the investigation was being conducted with his knowledge, the confrontation would be very awkward, for both of us. After all, in a revolutionary situation like the one we were in, anybody's political reliability could be questioned, and it would be wrong to act offended. And if I complained, there would be a very simple answer: "No one is following you, it is just your imagination; and if someone does follow you, it is only routine."

I decided that the best I could do would be to go on working, trusting in my innocence and in the justice of the party.

Then one evening, Thursday, November 24, the doorbell rang. I was at home listening to the radio with my son, Ivan.

I remember walking to the foyer and opening the door. The man waiting there was dressed in a leather coat with a belt, which was a standard uniform of the Czechoslovakian secret service. He showed me his identification papers. He was an employee of the Ministry of the Interior, and he told me that the Minister, Vaclav Nosek, wanted to see me.

Since there were some important things I had to do that night, I told the man that I would call the Minister and postpone the meeting until a mutually more convenient time. But the policeman insisted, saying that the Minister was still on his way home and that I would have to come with him at once.

Suddenly I knew that this was it.

I turned to my son and said good-by to him. I made the usual excuse: that I was being called to a meeting and would return soon. He went on listening to the radio. My wife would be coming home to give him dinner.

And who could tell, maybe I would be returning soon.

Outside, a black limousine was waiting. One policeman was in the driver's seat, and another was standing at the nose of the car. He opened the door and motioned me into the back seat. Then he and the man who had come to my door took their places on either side of me.

The car did not go toward Minister Nosek's house. After a few miles, we came to a roadblock manned by two armed guards. One of the men with me showed the guards a letter, and we proceeded on through a gate and across a yard to another gate.

Here the man again showed the letter, and the gate opened and closed like an iron curtain behind me.

I got out of the car, and one of the men said: "Mr. Deputy Minister, in the name of the Republic, you are under arrest."

Interrogation

Two guards took me to a small room, where they told me to empty my pockets and to take off my clothes. They painstakingly wrote down an inventory of everything I had, and then, while I stood there naked, asked me to sign it. Next they ordered me to open my mouth and checked to see if I had false teeth. Later I learned that prisoners had to surrender false teeth each night to their guards.

After they were satisfied that my teeth were my own, they ordered me to bend over and searched my rectum for concealed weapons or vials of poison. Finally, they made me stand, still naked, with my face to the wall, while they waited for their superior.

The superior read the prison rules. It was against regulations to tell anyone my name. If someone asked me who I was, it was my duty not to tell him. From this moment, I would be known only as a number, 1473, and I was to answer only to that number. He told me that this was for my own protection, for if my innocence was proved, no one would know that I had been there.

I did not know what to say to him. It was so entirely incredible. Ludicrous. When I demanded to know why I was being held prisoner, whether there were any written charges against me, as the law required before an arrest, I was told that all my questions would be answered by my interrogator.

Still naked, I was led into the neighboring storeroom and issued my prison clothing: underwear, a shirt, and pants that were too long, but no shoes or socks. They let me keep my own shoes, a new pair that I had bought in London just a few months before. As for the clothes they gave me, it was after the war, and everything, including clothing and shoes, was rationed. Even people who were not in prison were in rags; the underwear and prison uniform looked accordingly.

Finally, I was taken to my cell. It was after ten o'clock, and I was told to go to bed at once.

They kept the lights on all night, but I was dead tired after all those weeks of excitement and threat of the unknown. Now, with the tension gone, I fell into a deep sleep. I remember sleeping well for the first night in a long time.

It was six o'clock in the morning when they woke me. The guards told me to get up, clean the room, make my bed, and wash. They handed me a dustpan and a broom and showed me how to make the bed. It had a straw mattress and pillow, and two very rough sheets which had to be folded in exactly the right way; it took me half an hour to make the bed even after I got the knack of it.

When I had finished, I looked around my cell. It was about twelve feet by ten feet with a window very high up on one wall. In one corner was a "Turkish toilet," a hole with no seat. Above the toilet was a water pipe and faucet for washing, a piece of soap, and some sheets of old newspaper. Aside from the bed, the only furniture in the room was a small table and a chair. These were placed beside the large yellow steel door, which had a small spyhole in the middle of it.

At seven o'clock, a guard came to the door with breakfast. I could hear him put the metal dish on the concrete in front of the cell, and, a few minutes later, he opened the door just wide enough for me to reach out and pull it in. In those days, food was in pretty short supply in Prague, and real coffee was a precious commodity which fetched a huge price on the black market. The soupy, black liquid we got in prison was made of acorns and other substitutes. A single slice of bread was supposed to last all day.

After breakfast, I lay down on the cot and stared up at the peeling paint of the ceiling. Only then did I begin to think of what it meant to be a prisoner and, most of all, what it would mean to my family. When my son got up this very morning, I would be gone. What would he think when he found out that his father was in jail? What would he say, after all I had told him about my work, about the party, and about how I was working for a new and better world?

I suddenly remembered a scene in the spring of 1945, in London. I was about to join the Czechoslovak government in our liberated homeland, and my wife had brought our son to the railroad terminal to see me off.

The war was nearly over, and I had explained to Ivan that very soon he would be going home. After all those years in exile, he did not understand what "home" was. He thought that any hostel or apartment we stayed in was home. He did not even have a native language. He spoke German with his mother, had picked up a smattering of Italian while in Italy waiting for a visa, and had learned English in the Refugee Hostel in England. He did not learn Czech until the age of five, when we sent him to a Czech boarding school. Homeland? He did not know what the word meant. It was impossible to explain it to him. This fatherland that most of us grow up with and learn to love at a very early age: to Ivan it was incomprehensible, a fairy tale, a foreign word.

I had tried to explain to him where I was going, what I was going to do in Czechoslovakia. I told him that there would be no more war, that no one would be forced to leave his home again, that people would be just and kind to one another. And that I was going to fight to help make this happen.

And now I was in prison. It was all so incredible that I could only register what was happening, record it as a camera would, without understanding or really believing it. Why me? I, above all others, should know if I deserved to be punished. But I did not. And I could not believe that an examination of my record would reveal anything except that I accepted all my tasks in good faith and discharged what I thought were my responsibilities.

No. It all must have been a mistake.

There was a snag, however. A man like me, a deputy minister, could not have been arrested on some policeman's whim. The decision must have been made higher up—maybe at party headquarters, when they questioned me.

Mistake or not, it was the first time in my life that I was in jail. Worse, it was a Socialist prison, a prison built and run by a system I had worked for all my life, a system that had honored me for my work with praise and high office. I was more surprised than anything else.

Remembering that I still had my pipe and some cigars, I knocked on the door and quietly asked the guard for a light.

"Report!" he shouted. "Prisoner 1473 reports and requests a light."

When I had repeated what he said, he struck a match, lit my cigar, and closed the door. I lay down on the mattress, tasting the excellent cigar, and slowly started reasoning again. No, it could not be that bad. After all, I had a cigar between my teeth, and it had been lit by a prison guard. Everything would get cleared up. It was all a mistake. "Calm down," I said to myself. "Calm down. Collect yourself." It would be an uphill road, but my conscience was clear.

I heard an engine cough somewhere beyond the prison walls, then another, and still another. I could hear airplanes flying low over the roofs, and so I knew where I was: this was Ruzyne prison, the barrackslike structure near the airport that was directly beneath the path of all planes heading for or leaving Prague.

I heard guards opening doors and then voices, sounds of prisoners' steps reverberating in the corridor. Then suddenly I heard the very high wailing voice of a woman. She seemed to be screaming in pain and calling for help.

Then a plane came in very low and drowned out the voice. When the plane had passed, I no longer heard the voice. I wondered if I had actually heard it, if it was real. I did not want it to be real.

After that, nothing happened for a while. They left me sitting in my cell the whole morning. They banged on the door at lunchtime, and again at five o'clock, with what were supposed to be meals, and that was all. I was imprisoned on Thursday; Friday, Saturday, and Sunday passed, and I was still waiting to be interrogated. I walked up and down the cell the whole day with a feeling of absolute uncertainty, worry, fury, and desperation. But I also had hope.

In spite of all this, I slept well, possibly because I no longer felt threatened. The insecurity I had suffered before my arrest was somehow gone. I was only anxious to find out what charges there were against me. I wanted to be able to refute them.

All this is difficult to describe. When one suddenly finds oneself in prison, when one's life is suddenly and completely broken up, things begin to assume a completely different shape. It may also be that one sees and hears what one wants to see and hear. I may have heard those voices shouting for help, but I did not want to listen. Perhaps I shut myself off.

Monday morning, after I had finished washing, cleaning up my cell, and making my bed, the door opened and two guards entered. They handcuffed me behind my back and led me down the corridor past rows of cells like mine. At the end of the corridor was a locked steel barricade. There the guards turned me over to an interrogating officer, who took me through the barricade and up the stairs to one of the interrogation rooms on the floor above.

It was a small office, with three men sitting behind a desk, all civilians. One of them I knew: it was Doubek, who had interrogated me at the party headquarters. In the center sat a gray-haired man with a very narrow tie and a slight lisp. His name was Vladimir Kohoutek, and I was to see a lot of him over the next three years. The third man was a young Slovak, a former carpenter, who was Kohoutek's assistant; I have forgotten his name.

Kohoutek ordered the guards to take off my handcuffs and offered me a seat. There was a package of cheap cigarettes in front of him, and, seeing my eager look, he asked me to take one and motioned the Slovak to give me a light. The carpenter struck a match, and I eagerly inhaled the smoke.

After clearing his throat, Kohoutek reached for a file, opened it, and started asking routine questions: my name, my date of birth, my parents, my occupation, and my address. As I answered, he entered the information on a form on the desk in front of him. Then, without changing his tone of voice, Kohoutek began the interrogation.

He said that he knew that a few days ago I had been a deputy minister, one of the leading personalities in the country. Now, he said, I should look at myself and think about where I was.

Kohoutek had a very even voice, and this first time, as always, he called me by name: "Loebl. Loebl, sit down. Loebl, you are a traitor. Loebl, stop lying. Loebl, your cover-up won't work."

He continued by saying that I should understand that, since I had been in such a high position and was so well known abroad, this was not merely a police action. I would never have been put in jail if the very leadership of the party had not decided that I should be interrogated. And I should realize that I had already been sentenced by the party. Finally he said that everything depended on whether or not I would confess and tell them with whom I worked against the party and against Socialism—who gave me my orders and who were my associates. He said that my complete confession was the only thing that they were interested in.

I could not believe my ears. There were no specific charges whatsoever against me, only a request that I confess. There were no facts, no witnesses. Because I was a prisoner, I must be guilty of something, and Kohoutek wanted to find out what.

I told them that if they were so sure that I was guilty, they should indict me. Why bother with an interrogation if they already knew all the facts? Kohoutek replied that they knew I was a criminal, but that they wanted the details of my criminal activities, especially the identities of my coconspirators. If I cooperated, the party would be merciful; if not, I could expect the worst.

I lost my temper and shouted at him, "I have a right to know the specific charges against me!"

Kohoutek got up from behind the desk, walked over to where I was sitting, and shouted in my face: "Don't think that we are going to swallow your Jewish tricks. You want to know what *we* already know so that you can better hide what we don't know yet. Our instructions are to give you no information whatsoever; you will have to tell us about your crimes yourself."

I remember shouting back at him to take me to court and to prove his case there, if he could. I said that I knew I was innocent and that he had not a shred of real evidence against me. As far as I was concerned, there was nothing else to talk about.

To my astonishment, this worked. Seeing that I had nothing more to say, Kohoutek piped down and returned to his chair. His voice was like that of a teacher talking to a pupil.

"Everyone here is guilty, Loebl. We don't arrest innocent people. Loebl, we know you are a traitor, a spy, and a saboteur. If we didn't have proof of that, you'd still be deputy minister."

I did not know what to say. Again he got up and stood in front of me, and I could smell the tobacco on his breath. "Let me give you some advice, Loebl, the way I'd advise a friend. Confess everything. Now. Give us all the details. Believe me, Loebl, the party will be merciful, and if you make a sincere and complete confession, you will not be executed."

I told him that I did not see any reason for me to be executed.

He shook his head. "You leave me no choice."

He sat down at his typewriter, pulled out a sheet of paper, and started slowly pecking at the keys.

"You want to know what our charges are? Your whole life is a charge against you, Loebl. You have been an enemy of the working class and an enemy of Socialism from the very beginning."

He opened up a file on the desk in front of him.

"Loebl, I want you to tell me your whole life story, and as you talk, I will write it down."

I told him that I had already written a biography at party headquarters.

"I have a copy of it here in front of me," Kohoutek replied, "but now we want a *real* biography. The truth. With all the details. Loebl, we'll spend weeks on it if we have to."

Then Doubek said that he had also read what I wrote at party headquarters, but that they had discovered that all I had said was just an attempt to hide the truth and that a new "deposition" was absolutely necessary. This time, however, it would not be I who typed it, but the interrogator Kohoutek and his assistants, and I should be prepared to give them the information in as short a time as possible.

They would interrogate me in two shifts, eight hours each. After an hour of discussion, we began to go through my biography. Kohoutek told me to begin with my childhood, and I started to dictate.

"I was born in Holic, a village in western Slovakia with a population of about five thousand. My father was a merchant, and his father was a merchant. I was one of three children."

Kohoutek interrupted me.

"The most important thing in writing this deposition is objectivity, Loebl. That's what you have to learn. You have to learn to look at your life from the outside. You are telling me one thing, but whatever you say is always being distorted by the mind of a traitor. To get to the truth, Loebl, I must clarify what you say and write it objectively and concisely. I would phrase what you have just told me this way: 'I was born into a family of capitalists in a rural part of Slovakia, and from my youth, I was taught to exploit the working class and to hate their party.'"

I told him that was nonsense.

"On the contrary, Loebl, what you said implied all this. You deny your class adherence because it exposes you for what you are: an enemy of the working class. As you see, by objectively rephrasing what you say, I can show that your whole life has molded you to be a traitor to your party and your country."

I said I had left the village to go to technical school, that I had wanted to be a designer of machines, a draftsman.

"What you mean, Loebl, is that you were a careerist who went to a technical school because you wanted to boss workers instead of making an honest living as a working man."

I said I did not have the skill to be a good draftsman and decided to enroll in the University of World Trade in Vienna.

"In other words, your real aim in life was to be an unproductive capitalist who dealt in high finance and lived off the hard work of others."

Kohoutek asked about my family, and when he heard that my brother was a lawyer who immigrated to Israel, he immediately commented, "The truth is, Loebl, that you come from a Zionist family and that you are a Zionist imperialist yourself."

It went on like this all day. Kohoutek asked me about my life, but wrote down the "objective truths": that everything I had ever done was an integral part of my sabotage and planned treason. Again and again I told him what had really happened, but he never even bothered to write it down.

To have everything I said disputed, to have to wrangle with Kohoutek over every sentence he wrote down, was very exhausting work, but I forced myself to continue and not give in to his interpretations of what I said. I was convinced that eventually my superiors would ask to examine my file or have it examined by responsible comrades. They would do this because the person involved, the collaborator—myself—was so high up in the ranks of the party. It seemed to me that if I did not respond to the interrogation, however harsh it seemed, my position could be open to any interpretation. An attitude of indifference might even imply that I had something to hide.

And so I kept on refuting the charges leveled against me, however foolish or silly they appeared. I insisted that the wording of my "deposition" be as much as possible mine and not my interrogator's. I was terribly tired, and the wrangling seemed endless, but I felt that I was as successful as I could be under the circumstances.

I was frightened, but not of physical injury, as no one was threatening me yet. Very soon, I knew, my interrogators would want to indict me, or at least find reasons for an indictment, and so I concentrated my efforts on not giving away even the slightest point in my position and racked my brain for more and more material to defend myself. That was what my interrogators wanted—only I did not realize it then. It seemed to me that I was achieving what I wanted: to have the statement formulated more or less my way, not Kohoutek's.

I could not imagine that the President would not insist on reading my deposition, and I wanted him to read a description so detailed that my innocence would be obvious. I told myself that it was quite natural that such important evidence had to be written under the supervision of the appropriate organs of the party. If I had been in the President's place, I would not have wanted to communicate with a man under interrogation prior to having read all the relevant material.

But it never happened. Several years later I met a man named Sindelar, also in jail, who had been important in the Ministry of the Interior. He was able to give me the explanation.

While still in the ministry, Sindelar received a message from the Soviet intelligence service in Austria that said I was in contact with Anglo-American spies. I used to visit Austria because my wife's parents lived there, and Sindelar, in checking my background, found nothing wrong and dismissed the case.

However, he told me, Gottwald, Nosek, Slansky, and all the other important comrades were later given evidence that I had in fact been in touch with Anglo-American spies and had received sums of money from various sources in the West. This time the information seemed to be well founded, and they had no reason to disbelieve it, because it was always possible that indeed I was corrupt. Although I was not aware of it, the Soviet "proof" had made mine an open-and-shut case even before I knew it had started.

When the guards took me back through the steel barricades to my cell and I sat again on my straw mattress, I was depressed but also strangely elated. Now I knew that there was no evidence against me, that my interrogators were waiting for me to supply them with the facts in a confession I had no intention of making. I knew that Kohoutek had no real proof of any of his "charges," and I could prove all his accusations were nonsense. That was my trump card in any trial; if I did not lose my nerve and confess to things I had not done, I would have to win in the end.

It goes without saying that it hurt me to hear my interrogator making anti-Semitic remarks, which were obviously contrary to the entire ideology of the Communist party. I argued with myself that, after the war, with the party evolved from a small, select group of enthusiasts into a mass organization with a membership of almost one and a half million, it was natural that many of the people who were joining would have very different motivations from those of us who joined when the party was fighting against a powerful capitalist establishment.

In the early days, only those who were committed to certain ideals joined. Now, being a member of the party was connected with many advantages: advancement, position, power, even getting a job or higher pay. The leadership believed that the transformation of the party into a mass party was necessary for its successful access to power. Nevertheless, there were numerous discussions within the party about this dilution of ideals and the influx of so many new members not imbued with the party ideology. I myself thought that the years of Nazi domination during the war had imprinted a certain residue of Nazi ideology on the minds of the Czech and Slovak people.

Those who advocated a mass party always said that we must build Socialism with the material at our disposal; we would build Socialism and educate the people at the same time. As a matter of fact, the building of Socialism would educate them *ipso facto*.

In view of all this, even though my interrogator was not very intelligent and not very well educated, I still saw him as a comrade. The fact that he saw me as something very different was painful and disturbing, but this did not change my attitude toward cooperating with the party, or with him as a representative of the party.

Once, when I objected outright to his anti-Semitic remarks, he said: "Look, Loebl, we are not anti-Semites; we do recognize Jews who are faithful to the party. Why, some of our leading comrades are Jewish. But when I say a 'Jewish trick,' I mean a Jewish bourgeois trick. Despite the fact that you were a member of the party for so long, you kept to the spirit that you were educated in, and you didn't give up your upbringing, which was typical of Jewish bourgeois ideology."

Now I was ready to admit that, in a certain sense, he was right. When I studied at the technical high school, I was not interested in politics or social affairs. I thought exclusively of pursuing a professional career and achieving a good standard of living. When I turned to economics, I also had a strictly egotistical point of view. But it was precisely my study of economics that brought me to Marxism and into the party.

Kohoutek, however, wanted quite a different confession. He insisted that I just pretended to love the party; that, coming from a middle-class, bourgeois environment, I aimed from the beginning to worm my way into the party in order to corrupt it.

I said: "Look, what of Marx? Marx was also a member of a Jewish, middle-class family. And he was even married to an aristocrat." Kohoutek said that Marx had given up everything and devoted his whole life to the interests of the working class—which showed that he was not very familiar with Marx's life story—whereas I had no other interest than making a career.

So I said, "What about Engels, who was the owner of a factory?" Kohoutek replied that Engels was the owner of a factory only because he wanted to support Marx, that the need to supply the father of Socialism with money was Engels's only motivation in being a factory owner. He also said that there were naturally exceptions, but people who belonged to the Jewish bourgeoisie always tended to be Zionists, and Zionism was one of the tools of Anglo-American imperialism. I should confess that I was actually a Zionist, and that it was as a Zionist that I had wormed my way into the Communist movement.

Day after day the interrogation went on for sixteen hours without a break. Sometimes we talked through lunch and dinner, and by the end of the day, I was hungry and exhausted. Each interrogator worked an eight-hour shift, but I had to stay all day, answering questions, listening to harangues, and taking their insults.

They demanded that I sign every formulation on every page, and I argued about every sentence.

During the morning shift, Kohoutek did the questioning. He interrogated me about the years I had spent in England during the war. "You left your fatherland and let others suffer and fight the Nazis while you spent the war comfortably away from the fighting, living on money the British government paid you to be their spy. You indicated that yourself in the life story you wrote in the party headquarters."

"My passage from Warsaw to London was paid for by the British Committee for Refugees, and when I arrived, I got financial help from the Czech Refugee Trust Fund until I could find work."

"In other words, you admit having accepted money from British agencies, which means that you are a British agent."

I told him that the British committee helped *any* Czech refugee who wanted to escape the Nazis, as long as he could prove that he was really anti-Fascist.

"That committee and trust fund were a cover organization to recruit British spies. One of their spies, called Herman Field, was caught in Poland and confessed that you are one of the agents he had recruited."

I said that he had absolutely no proof that I was a spy, and that he could not have any—as it simply was not true.

Kohoutek quoted from my biography that, in the later years of the war, I became general secretary of the Czechoslovak-British Friendship Club, a group that coordinated Czechs and Slovaks of all political denominations and parties with their British friends. He said that I became its secretary to subvert that organization in the interests of the anti-Communist Czech group and of British Intelligence, who was sponsoring them. I told him that the club was a cover for the party organization in London.

"That may be true, but you intended to use it to sabotage the party and to destroy Socialism."

I pointed out that the Minister of the Interior, Nosek, was on the executive board of the club.

"Maybe Nosek didn't know. It is possible that you deceived him. We have proof that you have been sabotaging Socialism. You were appointed to a high government office by the bourgeois President, Beneš, who always has been a notorious advocate of the British and the Americans, and you worked closely with Jan Masaryk, who was also an enemy of Socialism."

I said that the Soviet Union had been the first country to recognize the Czechoslovak government in exile, in 1941.

"You are only trying to cover up your sabotage, Loebl. You were the Czechoslovak representative to UNRRA; you were the man who helped the United States, through its agents in UNRRA, to make sure that Czechoslovakia remained in the capitalist camp."

I replied that UNRRA had provided sixteen billion Czechoslovakian crowns' worth of aid when Czechoslovakia badly needed it.

"Aid? Is it really 'assistance' to turn your country over to its enemies? The truth, Loebl, is the object. The truth is that you came back from the imperialist West as their agent, determined to do anything to destroy Socialism in Czechoslovakia and turn your country over to the capitalists."

As we went through my "deposition," they wanted me to admit that whatever I had done, beginning with my childhood and my studies, was just another step in the development of an obnoxious traitor, of an enemy. They were constantly trying to add to my statements a sentence or two saying that my whole past was a precondition of my treachery.

However, I refused to sign anything that could be construed as an admission. I constantly insisted that only what I said should be in the deposition, and it seemed to me that I was achieving my aim. I thought I was managing to refute the charges leveled against me and, in so doing, to help expose the true enemy of the party, the unknown informer, and bring him to justice.

I told myself that I had to put aside all my subjective feelings, my feelings of injustice, because the party was fighting for the future of the world. Because, indeed, there was the danger of enemy penetration. Because I knew that such a thing was not only possible, but also most probable. When I joined the party, and during all those years that I was a member, I felt that any subjective element, any sacrifice, was to be borne for the party's sake. The noble aims of the party were worthy of that sacrifice, and I thought, at that time, that I was fighting for the truth and the very life of the party.

I acted in a very disciplined and loyal way, as I felt a good Communist should behave.

At this stage in my imprisonment, no kind of physical torture was applied. True, the food was very poor, but it was not a starvation diet. I was permitted to smoke, even during the interrogation. I had had some money on me when I went into prison, so I could buy cigarettes. I also had my pipe, and I was allowed to buy tobacco—or, rather, my interrogator bought tobacco for me.

Occasionally, sitting in the morning stillness in my cell or walking past closed doors, I heard screaming, as if people were being tortured, and the angry voices of interrogators. However, my attention was fully concentrated on my own case, on my own defense, and, during the interrogation—when the fight was on—I felt much more excitement than actual fear.

I realize, with hindsight, that this period was the first stage in the process of cutting off the world for a prisoner, by concentrating his entire strength and personality on the writing of a "deposition." And in his attempts to justify himself, the prisoner could provide his interrogators with more and more information for further stages of the treatment.

I told Kohoutek one day during the interrogation that torturing people, beating them, was against our ideology and what the party stood for. I remember I used the word "we," as if I were also responsible for what was going on.

Kohoutek explained that in the case of saboteurs, spies, and traitors, it was very important that they give up the names of their associates and sponsors immediately. He said that sentimentality was out of place in these times of stepped-up class war, when capitalism and Socialism were locked in a deadly struggle. The fact that I was objecting showed that I was nothing more than a petit-bourgeois liberal who would like to exercise restraint so that the enemy could win. After victory they would use far worse methods against us than we were using against them now.

A war, especially a class war, cannot be fought with gloves on, with restricted means. And White terror, fascist terror—in Poland, Hungary, Germany, Italy, and Franco's Spain—was infinitely more cruel than the terror used as an instrument of building Socialism.

What he said had a deep impact on me. After all, when Germany was being bombarded by the Allies in 1943 and 1944, I had inner qualms but I never protested officially; nor did I leave the party or resign from my governmental position when millions of Germans were removed from Czechoslovakia in 1945 and 1946 under conditions similar to those the Jews were subjected to during the Nazi period. Although these Germans had been living in the border mountains of Bohemia for centuries, and some of them were probably innocent, they were all being herded into trains. Each German—with a white armband on his arm— was permitted only one piece of luggage, with one hundred pounds of personal property.

What actually happened was that the values that Hitler applied in order to conquer the world had been, to a certain extent, adopted by his opponents. Far more bombs were dropped on small nations that happened to be in the realm of conflict between the great powers than during the whole of World War II.

I fully accepted that the fight that the party was conducting in the name of the underprivileged of the world was a just struggle. Those who owned the means of production would defend them to the bitter end with whatever weapons they had, and so, in order to prevail, the working class and the party that defended it would sometimes have to fight foul to achieve the final noble goal. Lenin had said, "When trees are felled, splinters fly." And hadn't the church burned thousands—tens of thousands—of innocent victims to save their souls in the name of heavenly love?

Even so, when I was in power and heard that people in our prisons were being tortured, I spoke to the Minister of the Interior. I remember that Nosek regretfully admitted that it was true. His explanation was that there were too many new people now in Security, that these people were radicals not yet sufficiently educated, and that we would fight against such extremes.

I confess that I became acutely conscious of the problem only when I was on the other side in prison. It is so easy to talk about revolutionary theories, flying splinters, and necessary victims, until you become a victim yourself. Suddenly you realize that it is not an abstract enemy who is being persecuted; the victims of the persecution are human beings, mistreated and crying out in real pain. When people open their newspapers at breakfast and see photographs, maps, and statistics, they do not realize the full human impact of what is printed on the page. Armchair strategists, amateur and professional, see armies as squares or shaded areas on a map. It is only when you see the dead and dying in front of you, when you hear the screams and feel the pain yourself, that you fully realize what war means.

There are also amateur strategists when it comes to revolutions—armchair revolutionaries. Some of them might be sincere. It is, however, terrible when these armchair revolutionaries get a chance to put their theories into practice, when they get to power and start to bend and stretch human beings on the Procrustean bed of their notions.

It is the essence of Lenin's teachings that the end justifies the means. Before him, the Romans believed it; so did the church. The party justified every action by this axiom. We were led to believe it, and we did believe it.

As long as I was convinced that our cause, the cause of the workers of the world, was just and humane, I understood that we Communists could be forced by the enemy to use methods that were very often contrary to our beliefs.

It was a most confusing and painful situation; what I had stood for and justified in the past now turned out to be against me. Yet the fact that I was not an enemy did not change the basic premise that Communists, fighting for a just cause, were entitled to use any methods. I still stuck to that idea, despite the conditions under which I experienced its consequences.

I said to myself that even if *I* was to be a victim, there had been such victims in all great movements in the history of mankind. It was sad to be such a victim, but I felt that I had to accept this lot. The only thing I could do was to fight for the truth and for my innocence. And I was completely convinced that if I were released, I would shake hands with my interrogators—my comrades—and tell them that I recognized that they were serving the party.

The more I thought about it, the more I was ready to admit my shortcomings, especially my problematic class background. I was not a member of the working class, but had been born into a middle-class family, and so my relationship to the working class was not the same as that of a worker. As deputy minister of foreign trade and before, I was relatively well off. I had a car and a very nice apartment, and I lived so well that I almost felt guilty about it.

My relationship to the cause of the working class was not conceived spontaneously, but only intellectually; my grasp of their suffering was primarily theoretical. And even though I sympathized with the working class and had dedicated my life to work for their cause, I was a member of the intelligentsia, of the educated middle class.

I realized, almost with shame, that after I had left Czechoslovakia and become a refugee in Britain, after I had lost all my property, I somehow felt nearer to the working class, and I felt better for it. Like countless other middle-class intellectuals, I felt guilty about my background; I wanted and tried to atone for my life of "luxury" and the fact that I had not been born "a worker."

I really had the impression that Kohoutek was perfectly convinced that he was serving the party by discovering its enemies. He may not have been sure that I had actually committed those crimes he asked me to confess to, but he was convinced that politically I was an enemy. He and all the other investigators were sure that there was a great conspiracy of Anglo-American imperialists, Zionists, and world Jewry, against which they must protect Socialism. They assumed *a priori* that anybody was an enemy unless he could prove his innocence; they thought entirely in terms of class struggle, and they were bringing everybody and everything into this polarized relationship.

When I told them that I had spoken with this or that American or British journalist, they wanted me to admit that what I had told him could have been used for propaganda purposes against Czechoslovakia. They wanted to impute a criminal motivation to even the most innocent conversations.

Each page Kohoutek or the Slovak carpenter typed had to be signed with the words "written, read, and agreed upon" and then my name. There was nothing in the deposition that I did not agree to. Sometimes I would tell them that I would not sign unless this or that word was changed. My freedom to do this led me to believe that I was being treated with a certain correctness. Only later did I realize that they were perfectly satisfied for me to write down everything I knew, and that gradually pressure was being brought upon me to add one or two sentences indicating criminal intent.

They were constantly looking for the smallest chinks in my

armor. One day, they asked me whether I was faithful to my wife. I admitted that I was not, and immediately Kohoutek wanted me to put down in writing that I admitted that if someone was unfaithful to his wife, he could also be unfaithful to the party, to the working class, and to the nation. Every small personal item was used to destroy me.

The first good laugh I had in prison was on Stalin's seventieth birthday. There was a big celebration, to which Kohoutek and all of my regular interrogators had gone, so my questioning was conducted by an amateur. He said: "Look, today is Stalin's seventieth birthday. You'll never have another opportunity like this to confess that you're a traitor."

Although it seemed that we worked at a snail's pace, every day five or six pages of that endless deposition were written. With it, the interrogator also wrote small notes, a sort of digest, and observations of what I did and how I behaved. One day, while Kohoutek stood in the doorway and spoke to a guard, I looked at the handwritten report and tried to decipher it upside down. I read: "Loebl is biting his nails; he is very nervous. He is very excited, but he steadily denies everything." This particular digest was only half a page long; sometimes he wrote much more.

Finally, after several weeks, we finished the deposition. On the last page, I added a statement against which I had been warned: the interrogators had told me that I would be declaring myself a traitor once again, and that I did not want to help the party even now, when all my crimes were known. In the statement, I declared that, apart from any shortcomings I might have as a human being, I had never acted consciously against the party; that I still considered myself a faithful member of the party; and, finally, that I was prepared to devote my life to the tasks the party would assign to me in the future.

The deposition completed, Kohoutek and Doubek left the office in an atmosphere of great excitement. I did not know what it could mean, whether I would now be released or whether they would beat me up. I was left alone for two or three hours; I even missed dinner. Then, at eight or nine o'clock that night, the door flew open and a guard took me down the corridor, but in the opposite direction from the stairs to my cell.

At the end of the corridor was another steel barricade. As usual, one of my interrogators was waiting there. He took me one floor higher, and I was left in a waiting room I had never seen before.

After a few minutes, they ushered me into a large office, where two men were sitting behind a big desk. On their right, sitting in chairs, were Doubek—who was to become the chief interrogator for the entire show trial—and Kohoutek.

One of the men behind the desk was balding and probably around forty years old. When he spoke, I had the shock of my life: he addressed me in Russian.

I was being questioned in a Czechoslovak prison in Russian by a Soviet interrogator, and by the look of it, these two men behind the desk—and not Doubek and Kohoutek—were running the show.

When the Russian spoke, he chose his words carefully, even precisely. He was dead calm, completely under control, and always disciplined. Listening to him, I had the feeling that he was incapable of love or hate, that for him, life was simply a matter of obeying and being obeyed, and that he was dedicated to masters who, as far as he was concerned, could do no wrong.

The other man, a Ukrainian named Komarov, had the face of a simple peasant, kind and jolly, and when he interrogated me alone, he always showed a good sense of humor.

I found out much later that the Russian's name was Likhatsev. He was one of the most infamous of the "Beria Gorillas," agents of the Soviet Minister of Security, Beria.

In retrospect, their insolence and self-assurance seem almost amusing. Seven years later, in 1956, both Likhatsev and Komarov were sentenced to death and executed. Not long after that, Kohoutek and Doubek were each given eight years in prison. But at the time, the world was theirs.

For a while, Likhatsev and Komarov watched me in silence, smoking American cigarettes. When the Russian addressed

Kohoutek and Doubek, he was more polite than he was to me, but he had no respect for them and treated them as underlings. Soon his gaze returned to me.

Likhatsev told me that the fact that I was in prison meant that I had already been found guilty. A man with my background who was guilty of the crimes I had committed would not be sentenced to a few years in prison; there was only one fitting punishment for me—and that was death.

He said that I still had a chance to improve my lot, that the death sentence could be commuted to life imprisonment, or possibly even to a shorter sentence in prison. And he warned me that they did not have to put me on trial. He said that if I confessed, there would be a trial as a warning to those who might think of doing what I had done. But if there was no confession, there would be no trial. It would be very simple to execute me here in the prison, and no one would be the wiser. And I should not entertain any ideas of trying to scandalize the party by recanting my confession at a public trial; this would not be permitted.

Komarov added that the party had proof that I was a traitor, and my behavior in prison just gave them the missing link. Only a traitor would behave the way I did, and he said they had ways to make traitors talk. Their job was to protect the party against criminals like me, and they would do anything—including "cutting belts out of my skin"—to get me to confess.

There was no point in arguing with them, but, feeling desperate and furious, I defended myself as best I could. I could not be as calm as the Russian, and in my excitement, I raised my voice.

I told them that so far no one had accused me of any real crimes, but that naturally some of the decisions I had made were mistakes. But then, some of those mistakes were unavoidable. I told them that they could have me executed if they wanted to, but that I was still innocent.

The Russian cut me off. "Have you read what Comrade Malenkov said?" At that time, Malenkov was first secretary of the Soviet party. " 'Ni oshipky ni oshipetsky': neither big nor small mistakes. The party won't tolerate mistakes of any kind. Every saboteur tries to hide his crimes behind 'mistakes,' and says that they are unavoidable."

I tried to explain to him that in foreign trade, it was not often possible to know whether a policy or an action was a "mistake." This could only become clear years after a decision had been made. I might have made mistakes, but without intending to. And whatever I did was done with the best interests of my party and my country in mind.

Again Likhatsev cut me off. He was very angry, but his voice still remained calm and cold. I remember what he said almost word for word.

"You are not a Communist, and you are not a Czechoslovak. You are a dirty Jew, that's what you are. Israel is your only real fatherland, and you have sold out Socialism to your bosses, the Zionist, imperialist leaders of world Jewry. Let me tell you: the time is approaching fast when we'll have to exterminate all your kind."

I remember choking in powerless rage while he calmly continued with those insults in his even voice. He said I was a traitor and a saboteur, and then he went through the whole repertoire of anti-Semitic insults the Nazis had used. I remember looking at Kohoutek and Doubek, and I saw that both of them were very nervous.

In his sermonizing, nasal voice, more like a singsong, Likhatsev reminded me that I could be executed at any time. Then he called a guard to take me back to my cell.

I remember that my whole body was trembling as they led me down the corridor to my cell. During the weeks when I was writing my "deposition," I lived in the illusion that if the party leadership read it, they would see that I was innocent. Now it seemed that it was all wishful thinking.

I thought immediately of the Moscow trials. I confess that for the first time since my imprisonment, I was frightened enough to feel that everything was hopeless. While I was being interrogated by the Russians, I felt a strange combination of desperation and fury. I knew that nothing worse could happen to me than to be sentenced to death and to die, and my temper and answers were born out of the courage of desperation.

It seemed obvious to me that some elements in the Soviet administration had misconstrued our striving to fortify and strengthen Socialism in Czechoslovakia in our own way. There must have been a difference in strategy between the two fraternal parties, possibly a misunderstanding due to different methods, different tactics, different national thinking.

It was possible that someone in the Soviet administration saw in my attempts to establish trade with the West a betrayal of Socialism, directed against the interests of my country. But the opposite was true, and I decided that I would stick to the truth as I saw it.

I was devoted to the Soviet Union, and I saw in her the first Socialist state of the world. But that did not mean that I would be uncritical of her. During my visits to the Soviet Union, I saw many things that I did not like. On the other hand, this critical point of view did not alter my feelings toward the Soviet Union as a historical force.

The Soviet builders of Socialism had had to cope with the inheritance of czarism, and the "founding fathers" themselves had been educated under czarism. It would take a long time for them to overcome their past.

Furthermore, after the war it was very difficult to distinguish what was a consequence of the failure of the system and what was a consequence of the war itself. I had traveled through the Soviet Union and seen how the country had been devastated: villages where all the buildings had been destroyed, train stops without railway stations. The terrible sufferings and sacrifices of the Soviet Union offered themselves as an explanation for much that was wrong.

In 1947, I saw the famous Soviet writer Ilya Ehrenburg, whom I had known since prewar times, at a reception in Moscow. He had lived in Paris until 1940. After witnessing the fall of France in that beloved city of his—an event that gave him the material for a rather long novel called *The Fall of Paris*—he returned to Moscow and became famous there for his very chauvinist broadcasts during the war. These broadcasts—not only anti-Nazi but also anti-German—gave him a special position in the Soviet artistic establishment, in spite of the fact that he was a cosmopolite and a Jew.

During that 1947 visit to Moscow, I met several Soviet writers in Ehrenburg's apartment who were all very critical of the regime. Ehrenburg was one of those people who always remain rather loyal, if not sober, no matter how much vodka they drink. He admitted that in his great country things did not always go the way he liked, but argued that it was "simply not an easy task to create a new world."

When there was a discussion about Yugoslavia, the Soviets insisted that all other Socialist countries should understand that their survival depended on the achievements of the Soviet Union. Without the Soviet Union, there would be no Socialism; the only possible policy for the smaller countries was to subordinate their needs to the interests of the Soviet Union and to coordinate their politics with hers.

At that time, I saw a very similar attitude in the Americans toward their allies. Obviously they expressed it in a much subtler way than the Russians, but the United States supported only those countries that were beginning to follow American policies. However, at that time I also believed that we all should see in the Soviet Union the center and the heart of world Socialism, and my difference of opinion with the Russians was only a technical one; I believed that allowing a greater degree of independence would bring more people into the Soviet orbit than would a simplistic, linear approach. So our difference was not a difference in principles; it was only a difference in tactics. I might be critical, but I accepted Soviet leadership without hesitation.

Now, in prison, I felt a double tragedy: I was in a hopeless situation, and the Soviet Union, my great dream, the advocate of humanity, saw in me an enemy. And I was not their enemy, not even at this stage, when I already knew, deep in my bones, that they were going to ruin me.

When I entered Kohoutek's office on the morning after I was questioned by the Russians, he was fuming. There were no more cigarettes, and I was not permitted to sit; I had to stand during the entire interrogation, sometimes with my face to the wall. I remember that he shouted, "How could you act so disrespectful in front of our teachers?" He called the Soviet emissaries "teachers" and spoke of them in a tone of deep respect.

Kohoutek picked up a sheaf of papers, my official file, and waved it in front of my face. "Our teachers say that you are anti-Soviet, and your whole life proves that they are right," he said. "Why did you try to tie our Republic to the capitalist West? Why did you do everything in your power to obstruct relations with the Socialist Soviet Union? Why did you use your trade mission to Moscow to cause trouble between our two countries? Why did you refuse to cooperate with the Soviets, even when Foreign Trade Minister Mikoyan personally appealed to you to cooperate?"

I tried to explain that the decision to trade with the West had been made by the entire Czechoslovak government, and that, in our negotiations, Minister Mikoyan had naturally tried to get the most favorable terms for the Soviet Union, whereas I had insisted on terms that would benefit Czechoslovakia. There was a conflict, but such a conflict is natural in any negotiation between equal partners. I said that I was no more anti-Soviet than Mikoyan was anti-Czechoslovak. We had both done what we felt was best for our countries.

Kohoutek started pacing the room, lecturing me as he walked: "Once again, Loebl, you are trying to hide your treason behind words. We are now living in a divided world, in a world divided between partisans of capitalism and of Socialism. If you were a true patriot, you would do what is good for Socialism, and follow the leadership of our Soviet comrades."

Kohoutek took every opportunity to emphasize the importance

of the "teachers." He boasted about how they were running the interrogations, and he stressed that the Soviet Minister of Foreign Trade, Mikoyan, was personally involved in my arrest.

This might or might not have been the case. Kohoutek could have used the Minister's name to weaken me. If I believed that a very high member of the Soviet hierarchy had personally ordered my arrest, I would recognize that my situation was hopeless and would stop resisting.

There was, however, one awkward incident in which I had been involved with this close friend and personal associate of Stalin.

In the fall of 1947, when I was appointed head of a trade delegation with the rank of a minister plenipotentiary, I spent three months in negotiations with Anastas Mikoyan, then deputy prime minister of the USSR and a powerful member of the Soviet Politburo.

Mikoyan was an Armenian, a small man, around fifty, with black hair smelling of patchouli, an Oriental perfume. He had the pallid skin of people who get very little sunshine, piercing black eyes, and a crisp, cold official manner. He fitted the Armenian national image perfectly: he was a very shrewd businessman.

His political power was very great. He was an old-guard Bolshevik, and there was a picture of Lenin's funeral in his office—Mikoyan had been one of the pallbearers. On top of it all, he was fully aware of his power, and his delegation was very tense whenever he was present.

Like all high-level Soviet officials, Mikoyan kept late hours. The Soviets claimed that that was the most efficient way to run the government: high state and party officials could leave orders for their subordinates, who could spend the whole next day processing the material and have it ready for their superiors by late afternoon. The real reason, however, was quite different. Stalin was a night-worker and frequently called on members of his government late at night. This naturally influenced working habits all the way down the line.

The first official meeting between my delegation and the Russians took place in the beginning of September 1947, in the Soviet Ministry of Foreign Trade. Even though my sphere of activity was much narrower than his, Mikoyan seemed more interested in the details of whatever we discussed than I. While I tried to concentrate on the major problems, he always insisted on talking about details.

I was later informed that, again, this was Stalin's system. Stalin did not trust anyone, and he wanted to be told every detail before he made up his mind. He expected his ministers to be able to answer any question on any aspect of any deal, and so they were forced to spend a great deal of time studying details. This naturally slowed down the already slow pace of all negotiations with our Soviet partners.

I proposed using world prices as a basis for trade, but Mikoyan rejected them, saying that we should negotiate prices and everything else as the friends we were. He said that, in his opinion, good will was the most important thing. For the same reason—mutual good will—I insisted upon sticking to world prices: without their guidelines, our friendship could be taxed by constant haggling and uncertainty about how much this or that item should be counted.

After his initial refusal, Mikoyan suddenly agreed with me. I was surprised, because he had a reputation as a tough bargainer. The same thing happened with the currency question. I wanted to upgrade Czechoslovak crowns because they were related to the world currencies, whereas the Russian ruble was set at arbitrarily fixed ratios by the Soviet government. At first Mikoyan was hurt by my suggestion, but then he suddenly gave in on this point as well.

My whole delegation was surprised. The Czechoslovak Ambassador in Moscow said that Mikoyan probably gave in on Stalin's orders. After forcing the Czechs to refuse the Marshall Plan, Stalin was eager to cement a friendship with Gottwald and obviously must have given Mikoyan instructions to conclude an agreement as soon as possible. But only a few days later we suddenly ran into obstacles.

Czechoslovakia needed grain desperately, and the Soviets wanted us to pay for it with steel plate. We were prepared to do that, but then the Russians asked us to reserve our entire production of steel plate for them. This would have kept us from exporting steel elsewhere and would have crippled our trade with the West.

In addition, they proposed to deliver the grain at the same time that we delivered the steel. Mikoyan and I both knew that it would take a year to produce the required steel, whereas Czechoslovakia needed the grain immediately. We offered to give them the steel in monthly installments, but we could not afford to wait for monthly installments of grain.

Too late I realized that Mikoyan could well afford to give in on the currency and the prices: now that we had refused the Marshall Plan, we were totally dependent on the USSR. He had the upper hand, and he knew it.

I met with Mikoyan a few more times, but there was no progress. The meetings were short and tense, and he simply repeated that we should accept the generous terms he was offering.

On November 7, there was a reception given by Molotov, the Soviet Foreign Minister, in honor of the thirtieth anniversary of the October Revolution. I ran into Mikoyan at the reception, and I proposed that we should get together again, in private. We were both party members, I said. Why couldn't we speak together in that capacity? He said he would see what he could arrange.

A few days after the Molotov reception, one of Mikoyan's aides came to my room in the Hotel National and told me that Mikoyan would be waiting for me at eleven o'clock that night. I could bring my interpreter, but no one else from the delegation could come. I was to be at the entrance of the hotel at exactly eleven o'clock, and a man would come to fetch me. I was to follow him around the corner, where there would be a car waiting for me.

With their attention to diplomatic protocol, the Soviets were careful to treat me as a representative of my government. But now that I was to meet Mikoyan as party member to party member, they applied a different kind of protocol. It reminded me more of a meeting between two conspirators than the meeting of comrades in the capital of a Socialist country.

After a short trip, I was ushered into Mikoyan's luxurious office in the ministry. He was very interested in the political situation in Czechoslovakia, in the positions of the other parties of the coalition of four parties that we had then, and in my experiences in negotiating with the West.

Finally we came to the point of our differences. I summarized the issues on which I thought we agreed and mentioned those on which I thought we disagreed. I saw Mikoyan making notes, and I thought that I had succeeded in convincing him to accept our terms. Suddenly, he said that he, as minister of foreign trade of the Soviet Union, could conclude only agreements that were favorable to the Soviet Union.

I countered that I understood his position well, but that Czechoslovakia could not conclude agreements unfavorable to her side. Argentina, for example, would give us better terms than the Soviet Union.

I saw him getting very angry. He flushed a deep red and said that, in that case, we should sell to Argentina.

Then I, too, became angry. I said that we wished to sell to our Soviet comrades, but they must also respect our conditions.

The discussion got more and more heated. He repeated in a monotone that he was the minister of foreign trade of the USSR, and that it was his duty to . . . Every time he repeated it, I got angrier. Finally, I got up and said that I expected him to keep the promise Comrade Stalin had made to our Prime Minister (Comrade Gottwald at that time).

We parted in an icy atmosphere. When I left, it was clear to me that he would settle for nothing less than getting his own way.

There was one other topic on which we did not agree. I had already discussed this topic with Mr. Krutikow, the First Deputy Minister of Foreign Trade, but no progress had been made.

Czechoslovakia was a country very poor in raw materials. With the exception of coal, we had to import practically everything. However, we were rich in one "new" raw material: uranium ore.

After the liberation of Czechoslovakia, an interim trade agreement between my country and the USSR had been signed, and one of the items included in the agreement was uranium ore. The Soviets had offered to pay for the ore on the basis of cost plus ten percent. My chief, Dr. Hubert Ripka, who signed the agreement just after he had been appointed as minister of foreign affairs, had had no expert on hand and was not aware that this agreement was extremely unfavorable to us. My negotiations in Moscow were supposed to put our economic relationship with the Soviet Union on a more favorable basis with regard to this agreement as well.

As we had agreed to base our trade on world prices, I asked to have these prices applied to uranium ore, too. The negotiations suddenly became very hectic. The difference between the prices offered by the Soviet Union and those I was asking for amounted to more than two billion dollars for the five-year period that our agreement covered. The Soviets refused to pay the additional money.

Although I was head of the Czechoslovakian trade delegation, I did not have the right to threaten the Soviet representatives. I could have told them that I would break off the negotiations or that we would sell the uranium ore to the West if they did not agree to our demands, but I was not empowered to do this. I decided to use a tactic whereby without directly threatening the Soviets, I would still make them aware that there were other possibilities open to Czechoslovakia, and in this way maneuver them into accepting our terms.

It was well known that the Soviets were listening in on every telephone call being made from their country to the West, and also on those to Czechoslovakia, Poland, Rumania, Hungary, and their other fellow Socialist countries. Realizing that, given the time lag, people would be in their offices in Prague, I telephoned Dr. Ripka, who was a member of the Liberal party and very wary of Soviet intentions.

In our conversation, which I knew was being listened in on, I informed him that since I could not make any progress, and as I had no right to break off the negotiations, perhaps he himself should consider coming to Moscow.

My diplomacy seemed to work. When the Soviet Ambassador in Prague informed his government that Dr. Ripka was boarding a train for Russia, the Soviet government put at our disposal a luxury car, with a dining-room lounge, four bedrooms, a cook, and two servants. I rode in that special government car to meet Ripka at the Polish-Soviet border and spent a very pleasant thirty-six hours traveling across Russia and the Ukraine.

I accompanied Ripka to Moscow. When our train pulled into the station, one of the biggest surprises of my life awaited me. Our Ambassador and his associates were lined up along the platform to welcome us, and the mighty Mikoyan himself was there with them, surrounded by representatives of the Soviet Ministry of Foreign Trade. On top of it all, Mikoyan was an entirely different man from the one I had met that fateful night. He was smiling, he embraced me, he kissed me on both cheeks, and he said, looking deeply into my eyes, "I'm glad my government has finally agreed to accept your proposals, Eugen Adalbertovitch. Now there are absolutely no barriers in the way of our friendship."

I could not believe my eyes and ears. It was only later that I learned that a couple of days after my phone call, a special envoy from Stalin had arrived in Prague and met with Prime Minister Gottwald. Probably whatever Gottwald had told the emissary made Stalin change his mind, and so he gave Mikoyan the green light to wrap up our negotiations.

We returned to our hotel, ordered vodka and caviar, and celebrated; in a very short time we were all drunk. I was particularly happy as everybody was patting me on the back. I felt on top of the world.

I remember that a colleague of mine, an old Moscow hand,

mentioned just in passing that "someone will have to foot the bill," but I paid no attention at that time.

From then on, the negotiations went smoothly, and whenever there were any differences of opinion, we got our way. Most probably our Soviet counterparts were afraid that if Stalin learned of a hitch in the negotiations, he would suspect disobedience to his orders. I remember that in a dispute about the purchase price of the grain, I told one of Minister Mikoyan's deputies that I could not accept their terms, but that I would accept whatever Comrade Stalin decided. He demanded a recess for half an hour, and—exactly thirty minutes later—he returned and agreed to our terms. And I do not believe that Mikoyan or the deputy asked Stalin's advice.

After another week of negotiations, the agreement was finally concluded. Mikoyan gave a twelve-course dinner to celebrate. Before every course, the Russians proposed a toast, and for every toast we had to drink a glass of vodka to each of our countries, to eternal Czechoslovak-Soviet friendship, to the just-concluded trade agreement, again to President Beneš, Stalin, our governments, our countries, and on and on. The Soviets stood up to these invocations, but my delegation was totally destroyed. I do not remember how we got into our cars and back to the hotel.

I left the Soviet Union convinced that if there was any disagreement between Mikoyan and me, it was only because each of us was trying to protect his country's interests. I even appreciated Stalin's point of view. He had promised to help us, but it was perfectly natural for him to do so in a way that served his own interests. The terms of the final agreement left no doubt that we were equal partners and that the Soviet Union was a good, reliable ally which respected Czechoslovakian sovereignty.

As far as the uranium ore was concerned, it seemed then that the Soviets would give in. Mr. Krutikow called me and told me that he was sick, but that our negotiations could continue in a month or so. In the meantime, he became deputy prime minister.

After the Communist party took over Czechoslovakia's government in February 1948, Gottwald told me that he himself would handle the uranium problem. Whether he did so or not I do not know. The fact is that the Soviets continued to pay only the cost plus ten percent, and by this time, Czechoslovakia, in terms of world prices, has lost at least three billion dollars on the deal.

The Turning of the Screw

After Kohoutek sent me back to my cell to think about the possible consequences of Mikoyan's interest in my case, I found things going from bad to worse. I was brought to a new cell, far less comfortable than my previous one. It was only nine feet wide, with a concrete floor.

After exploring it, I sat down. Suddenly the guard opened the door and astonished me by telling me that I was not supposed to sit, that I must keep walking. Walk, walk, walk, and nothing else.

I stood and gaped at him, and he repeated that I was supposed to walk. I did what I was told and began to walk. And I kept on walking. Even when they brought lunch I was not permitted to sit. I had to eat standing up.

The little spyhole in the door kept opening, and, whenever I stood longer than a few moments, the rough voice of the guard would urge me to move. For the first few days, feeling isolated and weakened, I obeyed. After my many weeks in prison, I had learned how to economize my energy, to save it for resistance or some other well-planned and useful purpose. Breaking out of the accustomed course, out of the strange inertia I felt, would have needed a superhuman effort. There was a new situation, but I kept on reacting in the old way.

However, after a few days, something clicked in my head—possibly because it was a Sunday, and I was not interrogated on

Sundays. As bad as the interrogations were, it was still better to face Kohoutek than to be left walking in that small cell. This walking—up and down, along the walls, in a circle, and up and down again—became so painful and humiliating that I could not endure it any longer. I sat down on the floor. There was no chair, and the bed had to be folded into the wall during the day.

When the guard saw me through the spyhole, he opened the door and told me to get up.

I did not.

He challenged me once more, and again I did not obey.

After ten or fifteen minutes, an officer came and had me taken to a dark cell. This one was even smaller than the one I had been in, and it had no window. The cell was not heated, and its concrete floor was ice-cold. After a minute or two, I realized that the pain of sitting on the cold floor was worse than the pain of walking, and I had to start walking again.

That night, I was brought only a very thin mattress and one blanket. They kept me freezing all day and all night. Once a day, at lunchtime, I got some soup and a piece of bread to eat.

The choice was simple: I could walk in the heated cell upstairs and eat three times a day, or I could walk in the small, dark dungeon, eat only once, and freeze. But there was no escape from walking anywhere.

Actually, it seemed to me that the choice was not whether I should or should not obey, not whether I should or should not walk, but, more simply, whether I would or would not give in. I knew that once I gave in, my entire resistance would collapse.

To withstand the pressure and keep on resisting required such strength, such concentration of all the resources I could muster, that I was afraid to weaken my resistance with more physical punishment.

Faced with the most powerful establishment on earth wanting me to confess, there I was—in solitary confinement with no lawyer or legal possibilities of defense—determined to resist. I realized that I must not allow anything to interfere with this purpose.

I tried not to think of my wife and child. To stay strong, I had to fight all my emotions, to harden myself as a boxer hardens his muscles. I realized that the main aim of my interrogation was to break my resistance, by any means possible, whether physical or psychological. I asked myself why I should make their task easier. Perhaps one day they would lock me up in the dark cell out of their own volition, but as long as I was able to avoid it, I should strive to do so.

I subordinated everything to this one aim: not to confess. It became an obsession.

I was a member of the party, a Communist, in a party jail. I felt very much the way all believers throughout history must have felt when they were put into the mill of their own institutions.

In the late thirties, Arthur Koestler, an ex-Communist, wrote his famous novel, *Darkness at Noon*. In my opinion, that novel is romantic balderdash. Written during the Spanish Civil War, it is set in a Soviet prison at the time of the Moscow trials. A dedicated Communist, Rubashov, serves as the mouthpiece for the startling confessions of those trials. His "teacher" is a fine, godlike, philosophizing commissar who convinces him that he must immolate his ego for the party and confess to the most abominable crimes so that the party can survive.

There was no such commissar in the real jail. My interrogators did not try to appeal to my relationship with the party; they just repeated, as if by rote, that I could not be a Communist because I was not a member of the working class, that I was a petit-bourgeois intellectual who could never have anything to do with the party, that I had lied when I joined the party, and that I was lying again when I insisted that I was not lying.

All of the interrogators, the Soviets as well as the Czechs and Slovaks, were simple-minded, uneducated, unsophisticated people, who could not convince anyone of anything. As a matter of fact, contact with them strengthened my resistance against con-fession.

Night after night, guards came to wake me up and led me

through the corridors to the office of the "teachers." There I faced the same accusations, threats, and insults every night—all delivered by the Russian in his cold, expressionless, nasal voice. The very monotony made it easier to withstand.

There were many other factors that gave me the strength to resist as well, despite the tortures to which I was exposed. One feels a strong inner resistance to confessing that one is a traitor, a spy, or a liar. To expose myself to all who believed in me, to my friends, my comrades, and my son; to say that I had been lying and pretending, that I had betrayed them—this was something so painful even to think about that it was impossible for me to conceive of doing it unless there were a complete breakdown of my personality. Also, there is one's self-respect, one's pride, one's vanity. Vanity was a part of my moral nature, and, in these circumstances, it definitely reinforced my resistance.

My ideological and emotional relationship to the cause of the party also helped. In my desperate situation, I tried to convince myself that I had a mission: to prove that all the charges had been concocted by the enemies of the party, both here in Prague and abroad. In order to sustain my resistance, I created an image for myself: I was a hero with a great mission, and I must fight as a hero would. It all may sound childish when related many years later, but in that type of situation, everything is reduced to basics.

One night, there was something new. The Russian wanted me to tell him about my treacherous collaboration with the "Anglo-American spy," Vlado Clementis. And I knew that at that very moment, the man the Russian called a traitor was in New York, representing Czechoslovakia as minister of foreign affairs and delegate to the United Nations.

I listened in disbelief as the "teachers" called Clementis, one of the most gifted men in the government, an Anglo-American spy. They said that they had proof of Clementis's treason, but they wanted a confession from me that I was his accomplice. I refused to confess anything.

The very next morning, at eight o'clock, Kohoutek had me brought to his office and made me stand—for fourteen hours—until ten o'clock that night. The entire interrogation was centered on Clementis: when did I first meet him, when did I recollect seeing him and speaking to him, what had he said and what had I said to him, whether this was at home or in exile, before or after he became the minister of foreign affairs. Even the most trivial matters were reported.

I told Kohoutek that both Clementis and I liked soccer, and that every Sunday we used to go to see a match together. He immediately inquired whether we bought seats or whether we stood.

Naturally the seats were more expensive than standing room, and when I "confessed" that I had bought a seat and watched the match sitting, he turned this into the following indictment: "You two had contempt for ordinary people and particularly the working class; you bought expensive tickets and sat with the elite and other capitalist parasites."

Later, he asked me what paintings Clementis had in his apartment. I listed the few I could remember, including one I liked very much. It was a painting by Sima, a Czech painter who lived in Paris.

"What was the subject of the painting?"

I described it as well as I could and happened to mention that it was a surrealist painting. Kohoutek had heard of surrealism and knew that it was different from the only approved form of painting, Socialist realism, so he added to the indictment that we preferred art that escaped into the unreality of dreams to art that inspired workers for the class struggle. This was supposed to be further proof of our hatred of Socialism.

Kohoutek also asked me about a certain conversation I had had with Clementis in London during World War II. At that time, Clementis had been the director of the BBC's Slovak broadcast in London. During the battles raging in Slovakia between the advancing Soviet army and the retreating Nazis, a small town had been occupied by the Russians, then recaptured for a week by the Germans. When the Soviets celebrated their reoccupation of the town, a lady of a well-known Slovak family was raped by some Russian officers.

The German journalists played up the rape in German and Slovak broadcasts, and Clementis was wondering what stand the Czechoslovak government in London—an ally of the Soviet Union—should take: whether to admit or deny what had happened.

I mentioned a conversation Clementis and I had had about this, and Kohoutek wrote down that Clementis told in a public place stories that were meant to discredit the heroic Red Army. When I pointed out that we had been sitting in the corner of a restaurant and talking in Slovak in low voices, Kohoutek replied that he was far too smart to fall for my typical Jewish tricks.

He kept up the pressure on me to admit to what "really" happened, but for days I continued to deny it, even though he repeatedly threatened that, if I did not confess, he would hand me over to another officer who would see to it that I did.

The only real physical pain I felt was in my legs. Standing for fourteen hours a day, every day, is very tiring and painful. I was not even allowed to lean on a desk or against the wall.

The Ukrainian teacher came around regularly to check on my interrogators and my progress. When he met me alone, he was always frighteningly friendly, as if I were an old buddy to whom he was just giving some good advice.

"One day you will confess anyway," he said. "So far, no one has been able to stand up to what is going to happen to you. It really doesn't make any sense to let yourself be tortured like this, when all you have to do is to confess."

I told him just as frankly that as long as I had the will to resist, I simply would not confess, and that I would not falsely accuse anyone of being a traitor to the party.

Each day, the pain in my legs got worse. During the day, when I was interrogated, I had no time to think or feel, and I was so excited that I sometimes forgot the excruciating pain in my legs. I was so tired that I slept at night, even though I had to keep my hands on top of the blanket and the glaring lights were never turned off.

But there were days when I was not interrogated at all. Being left "in the cold" was possibly worse than the questioning. In the endless boredom of my cell, I longed for the strange excitement of being locked in mental combat with my interrogators—however hopeless that battle might look in hindsight.

To hold my own, not to give in, became the most important aim of my life, the sole purpose of my existence. And then one night I was taken once again to the large office of the Russian interrogator.

He said that his patience was at an end. Either I would confess tomorrow morning, or they would make me confess. He spoke to me slowly in his even, nasal voice: "We want you to admit that you have been and are an enemy of the USSR and of Socialism, and that you are an agent of Tito, of world Jewry, and of the Anglo-American imperialists. And we want a confession and a description of how, with whom, and on whose orders you have done what you have done."

I told him I did not know what he was talking about.

The next morning, I was taken before Kohoutek. The session was very short.

"Stop your futile attempts to destroy Socialism and tell us about your activities and your accomplices."

I refused, and they took me back to my cell.

A few minutes later, a guard came in and told me to take off my shoes. He gave me a pair of leather boots and told me to put them on instead. At first, they did not seem too uncomfortable, although the leather was old and hard and they seemed rather narrow.

When the guard took my shoes away, I had the feeling of overwhelming loss. I had bought those shoes in London, and they reminded me of happy and successful days. Now they were gone, my last link with my former life. However ridiculous it might seem, at that moment I felt tears welling up in my eyes. I stared at the new footwear they had given me, and I did not move.

The spyhole in the door opened, and the guard said, "Walk!"

As I walked, I found that the boots were much more uncomfortable than I had thought at first. The leather was so hard that, after a day of walking, I felt as if I had thousands of corns. I wanted more than anything else to lie in bed and get at least one good night's sleep.

Finally, it was ten o'clock, and I went to bed as usual. I was surprised when, a few minutes later, there was a loud knock on the door.

The guard shouted at me to get up. From now on, he said, whenever he knocked on the door, I was to report: "Prisoner 1473 reporting. One prisoner present; everything in order."

I repeated it after him, went back to bed, and fell asleep. Ten minutes later, there was more knocking.

I got up and looked around. In my drowsiness, I could not understand why he was knocking. I looked at the door as if it would tell me what I was supposed to do. Then the guard yelled, "Prisoner, report!"

I remembered what I was supposed to do and replied, "Prisoner 1473 reporting. One prisoner present; everything in order."

He ordered me to get back to bed.

And then, ten minutes later, there was more knocking. And it went on, every ten minutes or so, all that night.

I usually sleep well, and very deeply. I even slept through the blitz in London during the war, and thus far in prison I had usually slept well, for sleep was escape.

But now the knocking and the reporting every few minutes made it impossible to sleep.

I was not the only one awake. Above my cell, there was an office, and I could hear someone being interrogated. First there was the angry shouting of the interrogator, and then the desperate screams of the prisoner. The absolute stillness of the night made the screaming and shouting more nerve-racking than during the day. The sharp glare of the ever-lit bulb stung in my eyes.

The next day I staggered like a drunk. I was sleepy and tired; I had fantastic pains in my legs. But hour after hour I had to walk and walk.

I walked as slowly as I could, but even so I walked a mile or a mile and a half every hour, sixteen hours a day. After having walked twenty miles, hungry and underfed, I finally took off those hellish boots that tortured my feet.

I remember how agreeable the coldness of the concrete felt on my inflamed feet. However, at the next inspection, the guard saw that I was walking barefoot and ordered me to put the boots on again. He said that if I did not comply, they would throw me in the dark cell again.

As I walked back and forth in my cell, the day seemed to have no end. Every minute was an eternity. There was a window, but the glass was very thick, like that in the roof of a factory. I could see daylight, but I could not tell if it was raining or snowing outside.

The days were getting shorter. It got dark early in the afternoon, and they would turn on that stinging, blinding light.

They gave me supper at five o'clock as usual. I had to eat it standing, and I knew that when I finished I would have to walk another five hours.

I remember moaning, which actually relieved the worst of the pain. I tried to do it so that the guard would not hear me; I was sure that he reported everything I did, and I did not want my interrogators to know how much I was suffering. It was my tactic not to show weakness.

The first one or two nights I had to get up and report, I did not sleep at all. After that, I was so tired that I fell asleep as soon as I lay down. Every ten minutes the guard woke me up, and I rattled off my report. Sometimes I was sleeping so deeply that I did not hear the guard knocking, and he opened the door and kicked me until I got out of bed.

After several days of being awakened forty or fifty times during the night, my hands started trembling and I had dizzy spells. My skin hurt whenever I touched it or washed myself, and I was deeply depressed.

They also began to blindfold me whenever I left my cell. At first they just used an ordinary towel, but then they began using motorcycle goggles covered with black tape. After he had covered my eyes, the guard took me out of my cell, turned me around, and, every few steps, made me turn around again, so that I would lose all sense of direction. Each time I was taken out of my cell I was blindfolded, and this blindfolding was the most degrading experience in my whole life.

Just before Christmas, Kohoutek told me furiously that if I did not confess immediately, he would have to spend the holidays with me instead of with his family. He said that I would be spoiling his Christmas, and that if I spoiled Christmas for him and his family, he would spoil it for me. All he had to do was to give an order, and they would imprison my wife. If that didn't matter to me, I could not expect that it would matter to him.

"If you stop this ridiculous resistance and confess, we will restore your privileges. You'll get cigarettes and books, and you'll be able to sit down."

The thought that I would be able to sit down again, or sleep, or read, was almost too much for me. I would not have minded spending my whole life in prison, if only they would let me sit down and sleep and read.

I had to decide quickly what to do. I could not bear the idea that my wife might be arrested, that our Ivan would be left alone in Prague. It came to my mind that I could say that I would confess, and then, after Christmas, they would find out that I had not meant it. That way, everybody's wish would be fulfilled: Kohoutek would get to be with his family, my wife would be able to stay with our son, and I would get a cigarette and sit down.

What I did not know at that time was that my wife had been arrested the same night that I was. As I learned later, she had been transported to the women's wing of the same prison that I was in—Ruzyne—almost at the same time as I: her number was

1475. After I was set free, she told me that she had been in prison for six months but never knew that I was in prison as well. They told her that I was still deputy minister, and that I had decided to abandon her because of her treasonable activities. They wanted her to reveal my crimes.

On the first day of May, they had broadcast the May-day parade over the prison loudspeakers. My wife's interrogator called her in and told her that, at that very minute, while she was rotting away in prison, I was sitting on the reviewing stand with the rest of the government officials. He said that I did not care for her any more. Why would she then persist in protecting me? He challenged her to confess my crimes.

But at that time, before Christmas, I knew nothing about Fritzi's imprisonment, and so, when Kohoutek threatened to jail her, I really believed that her fate was in my hands. I no longer remember everything that went through my mind, but I told Kohoutek that I would confess.

Kohoutek was ecstatic. Now that I had admitted that I was a spy and an agent of the imperialists, he gave me a cigarette, wished me a merry Christmas, and, for the first time, honored me by shaking my hand.

When I got back to my cell, I found a small table and a chair along with two packs of cigarettes, matches, paper, and a pencil.

I sat down. Nobody opened the door; nobody shouted at me to walk. I smoked a cigarette. All at once I felt like the richest and smartest man in the world. I had saved my wife and son, I could sit down and smoke—and what must I give "them" in return?

In a day or two, I would tell them that I had changed my mind. What could they do to me?

The next day was Christmas Eve. Ordinarily the prison food was poor and monotonous: coffee substitute, vegetable soup, and tasteless boiled dumplings for dinner. Once in a while, they would give us vegetables or a small piece of sausage, but all too often, interrogation ran through meals and I did not eat at all.

That Christmas Eve, dinner was a thick fish soup, fried fish, and a whole loaf of white bread. It was the first time in prison that I had enough to eat. I finished dinner and saved half of the bread for the holiday. I smoked a cigarette and put off writing my confession until the next day.

I was hoping that no one would check on me during the holiday, so that I could keep my privileges for three days until they discovered that I was not serious about confessing. But on the second day, Christmas day, Doubek came to see what I had written.

When he found out that I had written nothing at all, he had a fit. He shouted at the guard to take away the table, chair, and cigarettes. He even pulled a lighted cigarette out of my mouth, threw it on the floor, and stamped on it. He swore, threatened me, took all the papers, and left. He certainly spoiled my Christmas, but I guess I spoiled his as well.

After that, the interrogations became more and more painful, in every sense of the word. More than anything, it was the pain in my legs that seemed unbearable.

Some days, the interrogation consisted of only one question: "Will you confess your crimes?"

When I said I would not, I had to turn my face toward the wall and stand in that position for the rest of the day. During all those hours, my interrogator would read a book, doodle, or type something on the typewriter. Now and then, one of his colleagues would come by, and the interrogator would stand in the open door, keeping an eye on me and talking, though not loudly enough for me to overhear anything.

Standing in the corner with my face against the wall was humiliating, and it made me very depressed. Even more depressing were the documents they let me read.

A few of my colleagues at the ministry, a couple of my lifelong friends, people I had helped and promoted to good jobs, had signed depositions and denunciations in which they professed that they had always suspected me of being a traitor. Some of them accused me of having made trade agreements detrimental to Czechoslovakia and contrary to her interests. Every trade agreement naturally has aspects that are favorable to each side; no agreement has ever achieved everything that either country wanted. The writers of the depositions would pick a single item from a trade agreement and point out that it was unfavorable to Socialism and proof of my sabotage.

Some of those letters might have been written with an eye toward benefiting the writer's career. But most of them had obviously been written under pressure. I knew that it was very dangerous to refuse to write a letter when asked to do so—and extremely difficult for anyone who wanted to keep his job to wriggle out of that duty. It was also totally out of the question to write favorably about someone who had spent so many months in jail.

At that time, I did not think the writers despicable. I imagined that they had been summoned by the secretary of their party cell and told that the party already had sufficient proof that I was a traitor. And even if they had known me as a man of impeccable behavior, they might think that I had been misleading them, as I was misleading the party. I myself had been told that others, probably as innocent as I was, were traitors—and I had believed it. I had simply not been able to imagine that a party member could be imprisoned without having committed any crime.

This same logic must naturally have seemed valid to my friends. As party members, they would of course believe what the party said. And in those days of mutual suspicion, when it was difficult to believe that there was smoke without fire, everyone would figure that a man in my position, negotiating all those contracts worth hundreds of thousands of dollars, would by the nature of his job be a constant target for temptation.

Nevertheless, these accusations depressed me deeply. Although I understood intellectually how the letters had come to be written and tried to convince myself that it did not matter, I felt the effects of this systematic snapping of the links that had bound me inwardly to my friends and collaborators.

One day, Karel Svab, the man who had been in charge of my interrogation in party headquarters and who was now deputy minister of the interior, came to my interrogation. He burst into the room, slim and small, with an energetic, military stride. Without even acknowledging Kohoutek's obsequious greetings, he walked straight over to me and shouted nervously, "We aren't going to play around with traitors like you. We want a confession, and we want it now."

I was standing with my face to the wall and saw him only out of the corner of my eye. I told him that I had committed no crimes and that the charges concerning my handling of foreign trade were so simplistic that no expert would corroborate them. I also told him that I wanted to have the chance to confront my accusers face to face, in the presence of impartial experts.

I did not mean to offend him, but he must have taken what I said that way. Svab was enraged.

"I don't intend to be cross-examined by a traitor who has already been sentenced to death. Turn around!"

Before I could turn, he spun me around on those aching feet of mine and slapped my face six or seven times with both hands.

When his anger had subsided, his face turned a deep red. He was embarrassed that he, a deputy minister, had lost his temper because of a prisoner. Worse, he had done something that his underlings usually did for him.

Kohoutek was sitting there in silence. He had never slapped me.

I felt the physical pain for some time, but what struck first and hardest was the humiliation. That feeling remained with me for days, and I remember it even now.

One day, Kohoutek had me brought from the cell for interrogation, and, as usual, he made me stand facing the wall. Suddenly he asked me to turn around, and he said, with feeling, "You know, Loebl, I realize that it is difficult to admit here that you are a spy, a traitor, and a saboteur, but I've got to get you accustomed to it."

He leaned across the table with a friendly glint in his eyes. "Repeat after me: I am a spy. I am a saboteur. I am a traitor."

I said that I was not a spy, a saboteur, or a traitor, but he told me to repeat it, and that that was an order. I knew that if I did not obey an order, I would be punished with the cold, dark dungeon and one meal a day until I gave in. And so I repeated, "I am a spy. I am a saboteur. I am a traitor."

He listened, nodded, and ordered me to repeat it. So I said once more that I was a spy, a saboteur, and a traitor. And again and again. He had me repeat it almost a hundred times, but when he told me to stop, I said, "Look, I am not a traitor, I am not a saboteur, and I am no spy, and you know it."

With that, Kohoutek started screaming, and, as punishment, he ordered me to repeat it again.

On another occasion, he had me repeat a report about my negotiations with the British government: how I left Prague, how I arrived in London, who was waiting for me at the airport, with whom I negotiated. The narration of the story took perhaps twenty minutes, and as soon as I had finished, he ordered me to repeat it.

I realized that he was not curious about some detail of the negotiations, but that this was his tactic to break my resistance. I repeated the story and tried not to show him how painful it was to me. At the same time, I tried to find a way to counterattack.

I went on repeating the story monotonously, one word sounding like another, and I watched as he got more and more weary. I wanted him to become more tired from listening than I was from speaking. As I went on droning my narration, he suddenly asked for the guard and had me taken back to my cell.

These small victories were a tremendous boost for me, but they kept me from realizing how inexorably my jailers were depriving me, step by step, of my human dignity.

The interrogators made me repeat in schoolboy fashion that I was a traitor, a spy, and a saboteur; they made me jump up and shout my number, day and night, like a zombie. I did not even have a name any more. The whole atmosphere of the prison was so totally contrary to human dignity that what Kohoutek was asking for did not seem like anything special.

Once a man under interrogation starts with a certain strategy or tactic in his fight for justification, the strategy takes command over him. His initial stand determines the first step, the first step determines the following one, and finally he is so deeply involved in this or that type of attitude that he simply does not have the strength to change it, even if it were to occur to him that he should.

I know it must be very difficult for a reader to believe this, but in those days I still thought I would win, with truth on my side and all my energies focused on a single goal. I kept remembering my discussion with Gottwald, when he said that this would be Gottwald's, and not Stalin's, Czechoslovakia.

I told myself that there was a difference in stance or tactics between the two leaders. Not a deadly clash, but simply a conflict of interests such as happens even between brothers. I thought that my suffering would put me in a position to be of great help to Gottwald in his quest for a Czechoslovak way to Socialism. I rationalized it all into a great mission: I had to deny all of their accusations and, in doing so, help Gottwald in his attempt to go his own way, Czechoslovakia's way. The feeling that I could withstand the pressure and fulfill my mission was another reservoir of strength.

With hindsight, I realize how desperately I was clinging to the notion that my universe was in order. There might be some deviations, some mistakes, but basically my world was perfectly in order.

I never thought that I would change my strategy for resistance, and, indeed, it kept me going for fourteen months.

The routine of prison life made time lose meaning. Had you asked me then how much time I had spent in jail, I could not have told you. It might have been a week, a month, or three months. It could all have happened in less than a minute.

I lived like a phonograph needle in the groove of an endlessly spinning record. On one end was my cell; on the other—connected by a corridor I always passed through blindfolded—was the office of my interrogator. When I was in Kohoutek's office, I yearned for the solitude of my cell. When I was back in my cell, I found myself wanting the excitement of an interrogation, of a duel with Kohoutek and the others.

I could tell the days of the week from the food I was served, because the weekly menu was always the same. The days were getting longer, and from outside, through the frosted window, came sunshine, which reflected in a patch on the ceiling of my cell.

But nothing happened in my life. There were no events, no hope, no perspective. I thought that a man would surely die with so much time on his hands.

The Seminar

I found that I could think with much greater concentration in my isolation than ever before. It was a new experience to follow my thoughts to their ultimate logical conclusions without once being distracted by other people, other demands on my time, or anything around me.

As a deputy minister, I never had enough time. I worked steadily from morning until night, and I felt guilty on those few occasions when I was not working, as if I were cheating someone or something.

Now, in prison, I learned how to fill emptiness with an idea, with a mental exercise, with memory and concentrated attention. As I walked up and down for endless hours in my cell, I tried to create my own world of escape out of daydreams and thoughts of my past life, out of theories and ideas.

I had always been a soccer fan. Now I would recall a game between the Slovak and the Czech championship teams. I would reconstruct it from beginning to end, imagining myself to be the center forward of the team, dribbling the ball and seeing it flying through my cell, whose walls gave way to an open field. Or I was the goalie, trying to catch a hard kick. I replayed the game in my mind's eye, every play, every situation. I analyzed it and played it again, attempting a different strategy.

I had also been a passionate follower of the Davis cup matches in Prague. Now I relived those matches in my mind. As I played in them, I spirited myself away from the tiny cell into the open air of a sporting contest.

I tried to remind myself of my erotic adventures. My mind worked like a film-editing machine; I would picture a certain episode, stop it, run it back, run it forward again, analyze it. I tried to recall the details of women's bodies and of our love-making, and I was pleased that I had many happy memories to look back on. I would sample them one by one, and in those that were not so happy, I tried to determine what had gone wrong so that I could replay them differently.

I find it incredible that human erotic desire does not die out even in a prisoner being subjected to severe physical exertion. I was forced to pace up and down in my cell for sixteen hours at a time, and I was underfed, emaciated, and sleepless; yet my sexual desire was very much alive.

In the regimen imposed on me, a prisoner could not even enjoy the pleasure of masturbation. I was being watched every few minutes from the spyhole, and during the night, I had to keep my hands outside the blanket. Besides, being forced to report every ten minutes or so, I always fell into a dead stupor as soon as I got back into bed. Sexual deprivation was one of the most terrible things I suffered while I was in solitary confinement.

One night—a New Year's Eve—the guards outside seemed to be in a good mood: they were calling to one another and cracking jokes, opening and slamming doors. Suddenly, I heard a strange sound in this man's world, a sound I had not heard for a long time: a woman's voice.

In spite of my condition and apathy, I was strangely excited. I suddenly felt stingingly the full extent of being deprived, not only of sex, but also, and more painfully, of contact with a woman, of the satisfaction of seeing, hearing, and talking to women.

The woman in the corridor laughed and giggled, and I realized that she was flirting with one of the guards. She must have been one of the female guards from the women's wing, as no one else could have entered the prison.

I remember walking over to the door and standing by it. My

whole body was trembling. They were talking, joking, laughing. The guard shushed her. I heard the rattling of the keys, and the door of the cell next to mine squeaked on its hinges. I heard their steps as they tumbled in—and then nothing.

I strained my ears, an involuntary listener, a "voyeur" seeing only with his mind.

I thought I heard the thudding of their bodies against the cell wall. I heard their moans of pleasure. I heard—or imagined I heard—the rhythmic breathing of a man engaged in making love. I heard the woman moaning and calling out, "Emile . . . Emile . . ."

They had their ecstasy, and the guard stage-whispered, so I could hear it through the wall, "For Christ's sake, keep your mouth shut. They'll hear us."

The woman laughed an excited, throaty laugh. I imagined that she must have very large breasts, and I pictured large, red nipples pushing through the gray blouse of her uniform.

Then I heard the door open and shut, and their steps echoed down the silent corridor. Still I stood transfixed at the door, until the spyhole opened quite close to my face. An eye stared directly through the hole into mine, and the guard's voice shouted, "Walk!"

Like a machine, I started walking again. What I had witnessed reminded me that life was still going on outside my cell, and I became acutely aware of how separate I was from life and to what extent I had been excluded from it. For many days afterward, I could not calm down, and I imagined the couple's moaning again and again.

All this happened at a time when I had been "put on ice"—left for weeks without any human contact. I did not even have the "pleasure" of being led down the corridor blindfolded and seeing another face, if only the face of my interrogator, Kohoutek.

I can remember passing the time by pulling out those wretched pieces of the party daily, *Rudé Pravo,* which were stuck behind the lavatory pipe to be used as toilet paper. Walking around my cell, I read the ads or the leading articles, imagined various items that were offered for sale, and pictured myself bargaining for them. The fantasy of even so simple a human contact was enjoyable to me.

There is a kind of biological clock in every human being, and this is developed more strongly in a prisoner. Late in the afternoon, about five—I remember the time very well because we were always fed then—the energy charge of the human personality is at its lowest ebb, and I used to have deep depressions.

Only through the window in the interrogator's office could I see the world outside. I could glimpse fields stretching toward the airport. In those fields, the members of the agricultural cooperative would be plowing, planting, or harvesting—whatever agricultural work was in season. I remember standing there one day and listening in rapture to the sound of the tractor, the engine of which was beating like a heart. I watched the tractor driver going through his chore all through my interrogation and was deeply depressed when he disappeared and the field was empty.

I took solace in creating and solving economic problems. Economics had always been my hobby, and I was well versed in Marxist classics. Walking up and down through my cell, I arranged a veritable seminar on Marxist economics, Marxist philosophy, and Marxist social theory. I racked my brain to remember the exact wording of this or that passage in order to verify an economic conclusion and to justify my own theories and thoughts. I tried to kill time by giving lectures. In an imaginary seminar on Marxism, I created dialogues with opponents, inventing their arguments and determining the best answer to defend the Marxist position.

One day I recalled an episode that I had forgotten. In 1944, when I was in Washington, I was lodged at the Statler Hotel, at that time the leading hotel in town. When I came to breakfast the first morning of my stay, the hostess ushered me to a table that was occupied by an elderly lady and gentleman.

I remember that the lady seemed fragile and had a wistful, almost Slavonic look, and the man had a gray mustache and spoke the King's English. We exchanged a few words of courtesy, and, since my accent must have told him that I was not an American, he asked me where I came from.

When I told him that I was a member of the Czechoslovak delegation to UNRRA, we started to discuss the economics of the postwar world. He asked me what we planned to do in Czechoslovakia. I explained that, as the Nazis had so thoroughly scrambled all our eggs, it would be not only foolish but also impossible to unscramble them, and that all the large enterprises that were now German property would be taken over by the Czechoslovak Republic and become national concerns.

I explained to him in detail that we wished to establish our own kind of Socialism, in which small-business men and small farmers could be independent. In this way, we would have the best of both worlds. The so-called "Iron Chancellor," Bismarck of Germany, used to say that he who rules Prague has the key to Europe, or at least to Central Europe, its heart. And I told my British breakfast companion that, as far as I was concerned, the Czech and Slovak people would prefer to hold the key in their own hands this time. I told him that all the parties of our coalition government (in exile) were united on this program; that because no blueprint existed for Socialism, it could assume manifold faces according to the traditions and the geographic, economic, and cultural development of this or that country; and, finally, that I believed that Socialism would be victorious and prevail over capitalism.

During the conversation, the old gentleman objected to certain Marxist formulations of mine, labeling them old-fashioned, and I, in my turn, dismissed his distinctly Keynesian viewpoint. He criticized Marxism; I criticized the pragmatic economics of Keynes, who was merely patching up the old economic forms of life.

Thereafter we met almost every day to make jokes about each other's theories. He found my labor theory of value as formulated by Marx a relic of the nineteenth century; I made jokes about Keynes's efforts to revive the classics and bolster capitalism.

Then one day, a friend of mine asked me where I had met

Keynes. He wished to meet the eminent economist and hoped that I could provide an introduction.

Suddenly I realized who my breakfast partner was. All the jokes and criticisms I had made about Keynesian economics had been made face to face with Keynes himself.

When I joined him for breakfast the next morning, I apologized for having been so uncivil and for making jokes about his views. I told him that I was honored to have the opportunity to meet him. However, from that point onward, our conversations stalled. I felt inferior, and I stopped joking at his expense. After that day, I was very careful to come to breakfast when Keynes had already finished or was just about to leave.

Anyway, there I was, walking up and down in my cell, my feet in pain, sleepless, terribly tired, and thinking of the past. I reargued my discussions with Keynes, convincing him and myself of the correctness of Marxist arguments, branching out and elaborating my analysis, to overcome the gray, constant boredom and dull ache I felt.

One of the great problems of being in solitary confinement was that I did not have enough subjects to think about. I would focus on something, and then I could repeat my thoughts about it a few times to fight the deadening boredom. But there was a limit to how often I could go over the same thoughts about the same topic.

Reworking my discussions with Keynes was a new theme, and I went through all the arguments. At first, I compared and contrasted the theories of Keynes and Marx. When I had exhausted that, I began to analyze the roots, the basic assumptions, of Keynesian economics. I came to the conclusion that rather than representing a simple revival of the classics, Keynes's theories constituted, in fact, a modest reform of their teachings.

Then I applied this method of considering the basis for an economic theory, instead of analyzing that theory's validity, to Marx and his ideas. After exploring the roots of Marx's theory of economics, I went one step further and confronted the basis of the theory with the economic experience of the twentieth century.

This approach was different from my usual one, that of comparing Marxian theory with contemporary society.

The more I thought about the concepts upon which Marx had based his theories, the more disturbed I became. They did not match our world, and they seemed, at root, to be inapplicable to twentieth-century economics. Such thoughts were too unpleasant for me, and I tried to push them out of my mind.

In time, my thoughts and analyses themselves became objects for further speculation or analysis. I started on a problem and came to a conclusion; then that conclusion became the jumping-off point for more problems and questions. Thinking became a wondrous pleasure, a drug, and I became an addict.

And thinking, getting lost in thoughts, in Marxist analysis, was not only a pleasure and a drug, it was also a source of strength. I was like a devout believer who recites the rosary and assures himself of union with God. My Marxian analysis and the seminars I gave to invisible students steeled me against doubts, against any temptation to confess.

Reaffirming my positive relation to Marxism and to the party gave me the strength to resist the pressure applied by the interrogators and all the tortures they marshaled against me. I saw no reason, aside from a feeling of personal tragedy, to change anything in my attitude toward the party. I could not let myself see any reason. I wanted Marx to be right, and I drove away any thoughts that would make me doubt his theories.

As I felt my ego in danger of being eroded, I was grasping for a sense of pathos and meaning. If not the pathos of a hero, then at least the pathos of a martyr. And I felt both—hero and martyr—because I kept my faith in the party even under those terrible conditions.

I sought pathos, but I am not sure whether that was the mainspring of my resistance. I held on to the feeling of being a hero or a martyr—I think they are essentially the same—and one who was faithful to the party under any conditions. But I do not think this feeling was the decisive factor in my prolonged resistance. It was more the idea that my stance was set, and, like the needle in an endlessly rotating record, I would persist in the attitude I had chosen.

One day, the door to my cell opened and a prisoner who was serving as barber came in to cut my hair. I was told to sit down, and a guard shackled my hands to the chair so that I could not get hold of the scissors. While the prisoner was cutting my hair, I was not permitted to speak to him, but I could watch him. It was one of those rare occasions I cherished for weeks afterward—I was seeing a human being other than my interrogator.

It was also my first opportunity in a long time to look at a guard. Usually I saw only their eyes, when they were observing me through the spyhole. This particular guard was very young and had probably just left the army. Like all the other guards in the political prison of Ruzyne, he must have been fully indoctrinated and proven loyal to the regime. He was probably a working-class person who was put into a well-paid position by the party organization and was conscious that disobedience would not only make him lose this favored position, but would also result in severe punishment. On top of that, he probably regarded me as a dangerous, subversive criminal, a traitor to the state and to the party, who was getting his just reward. And even if he had sympathy for me, he could not show it. There was always the possibility that I would betray any such approach during my interrogation, with disastrous results for himself.

I was listening to the swishing of the scissors and watching my hair fall to the ground. As I moved, I suddenly saw that the hair was white. Living in my cell like a larva in a cocoon, I did not realize the changes in my physical make-up that the long imprisonment had caused.

When the barber left, I was told to sweep the hair into the lavatory. I stood and watched as it floated in the dirty hole, a white, sloppy mess. I could not believe my eyes, and I did not move for a long time. Then I heard the clicking of the spyhole in the yellow steel door, and the rasping voice of the guard ordering me to get moving again.

Summer came, and nothing changed. Once every week or ten

days, the interrogator would call me to his office, have me stand there with my face to the wall for both shifts, and appeal to me or harangue me to confess. When I said I would not confess and that ultimately I would prove my innocence, he had me continue to stand there while he read a book in silence. I would look out of the corner of my eye through the window, seeing the sun and the blue sky and the fields outside and listening to the planes roaring low over the roof of the prison. One day, Kohoutek caught me at it; he made me turn to face the corner, shutting off even that avenue of escape.

I was terribly angry and unhappy. It is a strange feeling to be completely helpless. One feels like a worm that is being crushed by a big boot, like a cockroach trodden on by a giant.

But I also became conscious of my own power, the power of the prisoner. True, a prisoner is helpless; he has no freedom whatsoever. On the one hand, constantly hungry and sleepless, he is enclosed in a stone cell in a cement desert surrounded by human machines, and he has to stand, to walk, to do whatever he is ordered. But, on the other hand, he is constantly observed and reported on, a person of great importance.

I knew that Kohoutek was trying to sell me a confession, and I was not willing to buy it. I knew that his career depended on whether he could make me surrender, and I had decided not to give him that triumph. That was my strength, that and my belief in the ultimate justice of my stance, my firm belief in the Marxian foundations on which I had built my career.

In this void, where the prisoner is divorced from everything—family, reality, life itself—and where nothing exists, everything boils down to the strange relationship between the prisoner and his interrogator. Feeling so terribly humiliated, I believed that by denying everything, I was humiliating my interrogator. However, as much as I hated Kohoutek, he was still the only human being I had any contact with. I hated his guts, but it was better to be in his office, even if he offended me, called me names, and humiliated me, than to be left in my cell by myself, facing those merciless enemies of every prisoner, time and boredom.

When left in my cell, sometimes for weeks, without being interrogated or seeing any human face except that single eye in the spyhole, I was really longing to be interrogated again. I wanted to speak to another human being, to assert my personality with him, to shout in his face that I was innocent, that I would never confess or lie. And I would enjoy seeing his fury.

But when I was interrogated for hours at a stretch, I was desperately longing for the solitude of my cell, where I would not have to see Kohoutek's pudgy face.

As it is in life, so it is in prison: things are never just black and white. It would be false to describe the relationship between a prisoner and his interrogator in simplistic terms. Just as Kohoutek was the only person in my life for two years or more, my persistence, my personality, and my psyche must have been the center of the universe for him as well. Our meetings were duels, clashings of minds, and when he had me walk painfully for weeks and months in my cell without interrogating me, I consoled myself with the idea that when we did meet again, he would not be one iota nearer triumph.

Kohoutek and all the other interrogators were impregnated with a feeling of tremendous arrogance. How superior they must have felt, not only to us prisoners, but also to all other citizens. They must have felt drunk with power.

Many months later, when Kohoutek was preparing me for the confrontation with the already imprisoned Slansky, I saw his body move and twitch as if in an orgastic spasm. At the time of my imprisonment, Rudolf Slansky had been general secretary of the party, and thus held tremendous power. In this function he stood above the law; as a matter of fact, he was the law. When Kohoutek told me that "that bastard Slansky" was now going to confess, he rubbed his thighs and moistened his lips. It was indeed an orgasm of power: the General Secretary of the party, the man who used to be his god, was now in his hands.

The interrogators would speak of ministers who were still in office—Jaromir Dolansky, Minister of Finance; Nosek, Minister of the Interior; even the Prime Minister, Antonin Zapotocky—with voracious anticipation, like beasts in a zoo eagerly awaiting the carcasses that would be thrown to them before long. They knew that any one of those men might end up in prison, and that he would confess sooner or later. And *they* would be the ones who would force him to say whatever *they* wanted. These men, some of whom could hardly read and write, were suddenly potential rulers of the country.

This sense of power also gave them patience. It did not matter whether a prisoner confessed in a month, three months, or a year. It did not matter whether I would be sentenced in the next four months or the next two years; I could even die in prison. They could wait. Having the certainty that everyone would confess sooner or later, they knew that time was not their enemy, but their ally.

They had been taught to know time as their ally and the prisoner's enemy. And with almost unlimited time at their disposal, they foresaw and planned what was to come. This planning and thinking in terms of time is a peculiarly Russian, or Eastern, quality. The same element can be discerned in the foreign policy of the Soviet Union. Whatever the Russians do, they consider time expendable.

There I was in the strange, timeless world of the prison. I walked up and down and around in my cell, trying to think or not to think, trembling with pain, feeling that I must not give in, that I simply could not collapse. And I tried not to think of my son or of my wife.

Thinking about them made my resistance weaken, but pushing them out of my mind was not an easy task. I could not help thinking about them from time to time, and I had an overwhelming desire to hear from them, to get a letter, a few lines at least. I suffered from what had happened to me, but it was even more unendurable not to know how my wife and child were, to fear that they might be drawn into the abyss with me.

Several times during my imprisonment I asked for permission

to write to them. When Kohoutek told me that I would only get permission to write a letter to my wife after I had confessed, I told him that even in Nazi concentration camps, people were permitted to write letters. The fact that I compared him to an SS man, and Socialist prisons to concentration camps, was more than he could bear. He jumped up from behind his desk and started calling me names like "swine," "traitor," and "arrogant Jew," and finally he said:

"Look, Loebl, if you loved your son and your wife you would confess. But you love those people who gave you money to betray your country even more. You are ready to betray the interests of your child for your associates, for your backers; and on top of it, you put the blame on us. Do you know what you are? You, you yourself, Loebl, are a fascist, a Gestapo man."

When I returned to my cell, I was even more tense and excited than usual. In a strange way, I felt that Kohoutek was right. Yes, I had betrayed my son for the sake of the party. For the great cause, I had sacrificed my private life. Instead of taking Ivan to a theater or out to a soccer game, I would tell him that I had an important meeting. I suddenly felt that I had not been a good father to my son. And I recognized that for me, a relationship between human beings had been far too much of an ideological issue.

It was not the relationship of man to man, but, rather, the relationship of man to man through an ideology that I had experienced. How was it possible that Marxist humanism and my belief in it had made me less human than I should have been?

The Party

When I thought about the possibility of being released from prison, I knew that I would continue as before. My membership in the party had been part of my personality, a mission. The desire to fulfill this mission had become a deeply rooted passion with me.

In the days when the Communist party was small, facing the police and the administrative apparatus of the powerful capitalist establishment, membership in the party was politically, socially, and materially full of disadvantages. Only people who were ready to face political persecution and loss of employment and who were willing to pay heavy party dues would join, but in those days being a member meant joining a group of people who had intellectual honesty, great decency, and extreme loyalty to one another. The feeling that we were siding with the underdogs, with the oppressed working class of the world, against capitalists, compensated us for the material disadvantages.

As a student in Vienna, I witnessed the stormy rise of the Nazi movement. Large sections of the German and Austrian middle class not only did nothing to prevent the spread of this venom, but also actually financed and helped Hitler and his party. Mussolini invaded small and valiant Abyssinia and used gas on the primitive warriors of the Harari tribe, but the rich, powerful Western democracies could not bring themselves to interfere.

I experienced the Great Depression. My small country of barely fifteen million people had almost a million unemployed, and no one knew what measures to take to alleviate that blight. The economy seemed to go from bad to worse, and there was the sense of a great crisis looming in the near future. It became obvious that Hitler was preparing for war, and yet nothing was done to prevent that war; country after country was being sacrificed.

When I was young, I believed that Freemasonry might offer a solution to the chaos I saw around me, and I joined a Freemason lodge. Mine was called "Harmonia" and had its center in Hamburg, Germany. It was a "reformed lodge," not a traditional one, in that our ceremonies were reduced to a minimum and never played an important part in our meetings. However, I soon discovered that my lodge was only a kind of social club, where middle-class people could meet and support one another's views, with a bit of moral uplift thrown in.

I was disappointed with every feature of the establishment—its ideology, its code of behavior, and now its Freemasonry. I soon drifted away and joined the first so-called Ethical Movement and later the Social Democratic party. I found that the Ethical Movement devoted itself only to discussions and shunned action, and that the Social Democrats were busily collaborating with the very interests they should have fought.

I was living at a time when, through inflation and depression, millions of people lost everything they had ever owned while those in one social stratum, the owners of the means of production, were waxing richer and richer. None of the conventional economic theories offered any meaningful answers to these terrible problems. They were concerned with definitional statements and empty concepts in no way related to what was happening. Sterile discussions like those of medieval scholars could be heard: is the Depression the consequence of overproduction or underconsumption? But there was no attempt to find solutions to the current economic problems. In this climate of economic crisis and the growing threat of fascism, I made the decision to turn to Marxism.

What fascinated me then about Marx, and still does, was that his concern was not to interpret the world, but to change it. He taught that the responsibility lies with the system and not with the individual, not even with the individual capitalist. And in order to change the system and direct it toward humane goals, we would need to use the tool of social science.

Marx blamed the conflict between private ownership, on the one hand, and collective production, on the other, for all the evils of the capitalist society. In this type of society, profit became God, and the common good was sacrificed to it.

I saw myself in a world where milk was being dumped into the sewers and cattle were slaughtered and dumped into pits; where mines were overstocked with coal, and wheat was burned up in furnaces; where factories stood idle while the unemployed filled the streets. In this madness that passed for an economy, Marx offered me an explanation and a solution.

What could be simpler than to expropriate all the means of production, which were run for profit, and run them for the benefit of society as a whole? Such a society, where the means of production—the mines, the factories, and the fields—would belong to and be controlled by the community, would be called the Socialist society, and the system itself, Socialism.

Within this scheme, all the missing pieces fell into place. It presented me, as it did many others, with a real perspective for a better world. The chaotic life I was witnessing could be regulated if only we could expropriate the means of production and apply them to the service of whole nations, of the entire community.

Naturally, the former owners who were living on the profits would not give up without a fight. As I saw it then, they were actually fighting already, on a united front which was world-wide. In Germany, they had armed Hitler; in Italy, they helped Mussolini. And there was only one way to get rid of them: the revolutionary way.

The revolution could not happen peacefully. It would need a class, a huge body, to fight and achieve the transfer. There was one such class, one stratum of society, that could undertake such a revolution; one force that was historically destined to achieve this goal. They were the ones exploited by the capitalists and in whose interest it would be to take over the means of production: the working class.

And the working class had to be organized, steeled, and prepared for this great purpose. For this reason, it was necessary to create a party that would be their vanguard and leader. Lenin, half a century before, had created such a party, the Communist party, which had managed to come to power in one country of the world, the Soviet Union. This was why we saw the great fulfillment of our ideas in the Soviet Union; it was the laboratory where the restructuring of society was being put into practice. In the words of Lincoln Steffens: "I saw the future, and it works." For the moment, it was not important how.

For the first time, as we saw it, the underprivileged of the world had control of the means of production; now they would establish that kind of society, that kind of state, where the social benefits would be distributed according to everyone's contribution.

It was clear to us that the past of Russia—the czarist regime, the backwardness, the lack of democratic traditions—had created distortions in the original Socialist doctrine as put into practice in the Soviet Union. But having the choice of an imperfect Socialist country or none at all, we voted hands down for the Soviet Union and defended her against all charges, even though we knew that some of them might be justified.

It seemed to us that—exactly as Marx and Lenin had predicted—big monopolies, private and corporate, would invest in those men and movements who would guarantee their continued rule and continued profits. Faced with the choice of either Socialism or fascism, the capitalists would inevitably side with the dictators, with Mussolini in Italy and Hitler in Germany. And we wanted to prevent this.

There were two forces exerting a strain on the established social order in those days. One was a merciless depression that harmed almost everyone; the other was that no alternatives to the current social order existed but National Socialism, advocated by

Hitler, and Marxist Socialism. Under the impact of these two pressures, the basis of democratic capitalism was weakening day by day.

And as I write this, forty years later, the very same dreams and views are spreading all over the world. Again, a social system dominated by the interests of a few is in crisis, but we have no humanistic alternative to that system. And again, conventional economics, whose only answer is the justification of a trade-off between employment and inflation, has no real perspective and shows no real concern for human beings. Despite all the bitter experience with applied Marxism, the absence of a humane economic science with concrete solutions to today's problems causes us to witness a renaissance of Marxism.

When I entered the ranks of the party, I worked with them for a year or two before formally becoming a member. I was what is called a sympathizer, but I paid my dues and took on tasks assigned to me by the party organization. I stuck up posters, wrote articles, gave lectures, and ran seminars.

My devotion to the party and its cause before I actually became a member made my formal entrance into the Communist ranks a matter of course. I regarded myself as a party member even before I actually got my card. And my duties did not really change with official membership, they only broadened. I became an editor on the staff of a Marxist monthly founded by Clementis called *Dav* (The Crowd). I held Marxist seminars for university students, wrote theoretical articles, lectured on the Soviet economy, and attended meetings of political opponents of Communism in order to defend Marx and his theories. Step by step, my whole life became absorbed by these political activities.

At last I had found an organization that seemed to be doing something to combat the social ills of our day. Unlike the other groups I had joined, the party was an activist organization. In addition to my other work, I took part in demonstrations in support of strikes and, along with my comrades, was frequently beaten up by police truncheons. Sometimes we would pull the policemen from their horses by their sabers, and it was great fun to see them fall down on the pavement like so many bowling pins. We also visited workers' organizations once or twice a week. I remember being invited to workers' homes and how open and eager the workers were for encouragement and instruction. They were committed to our ideas and desperately wanted to become enlightened.

And the party was more than an organization. It called for commitment of the whole man, and the man, in his turn, absorbed the party. It demanded more sacrifices than a church. The party appealed not only to the emotions, but to the intellect as well.

I could travel all over Czechoslovakia and enter any apartment of any party comrade, and it was as if I were a member of his family. It was a brotherhood, a kind of Knighthood of the Holy Grail. It was a wonderful life, with no alienation or frustration, only a passionate belief in the future and a deep-rooted optimism.

No. I had no reason to change anything. I could not be shaken in my faith just because I had had the misfortune to become the victim of something I could not understand, just because a bunch of opportunists and gangsters had got to the helm of the party and the state. All those circumstances were mysterious to me and made me feel wretched, but they did not change my basic ideology.

It was, as I said before, this faith, this strong belief in the party, that enabled me to resist Kohoutek as long as I did. If his methods had changed my attitude toward the party as quickly as he wished, my relationship with it would have had to be very superficial indeed.

A year had passed since I had been arrested and put in jail. I continued to walk up and down in my cell, and the guard continued to open the spyhole every few minutes to check on me. My two interrogators continued to write their observations on half a sheet of paper that was immediately whisked away to the Russian or the Ukrainian somewhere in the depths of the prison.

Once or twice, the Ukrainian came in while I was being interrogated or while I stood facing the wall. He would click his tongue, shake his head, and poke me in the back in rather friendly fashion.

"Still resisting? Better confess and spare yourself a lot of trouble. If you don't confess now, you'll confess tomorrow, but you'll confess anyway."

And when I would blurt out, now almost in tears, that I had nothing to confess, that I was innocent, he would shrug his shoulders and mutter under his breath that I was a *durak*—an idiot—and walk away with his sailor's swagger.

The Death Sentence

With each of us sitting in his individual cell, the prison was like a giant concrete honeycomb. There was not the slightest chance to succeed in a revolt, for we were never together: it was always one isolated prisoner against many interrogators and guards. There was no possibility of ganging up, and certainly no possibility of imbuing one another with strength or solidarity. We were all alone and terribly lonely. There was no way out except to fight it out with the interrogator or die.

And so, one afternoon, when my faith was at its lowest ebb and I was walking around the cell like a drunk, I said to myself that I should just get out. Quit. Commit suicide.

It was not a dramatic decision. I simply made up my mind that it would be better to stop living. With this decision came a very difficult question, namely, how could I commit suicide in my present situation? It was impossible to cut my wrists or bite my veins open, as I was being observed every five or ten minutes during the day, and at night my hands had to be outside the blanket. The simplest way seemed to be starvation. I would throw my meals into the lavatory and wait. I was so exhausted that I knew it would not take me long to die, and since I was practically a skeleton, maybe they would not even notice what I was doing until it was too late.

When dinner came, I waited until the guard had gone to the next cell. Then I went to the lavatory, threw in the food I craved, and pulled the chain.

At the sound of running water, the guard rushed toward my

cell, shouting that I was not supposed to use the lavatory during meals. He said that if I did it again I would go to the dark cell.

The incident must have been reported to Kohoutek. During the next interrogation he smirked and said that I should not hope to escape punishment by a hunger strike. If necessary, they would force-feed me, or feed me intravenously.

When I returned to my room, I tried to think up another method. It occurred to me that I could possibly use dust as poison. I decided to bite into my hands and rub dust in the wounds; if I was lucky, I would get blood poisoning.

I collected dust in the corner by the lavatory, so that when the cell was inspected it would not be seen, and started to bite my fingers around the nails.

I bit them until they bled and then rubbed a large amount of dust into the wounds. It was painful to repeat this process day after day, especially after one or two fingers became infected, but I continued.

The infected fingers became swollen and full of pus; they ached badly. I remember walking up and down in my cell, in terrible desperation. The pain was almost unbearable, but I continued to bite the nails and the skin of my fingers. I used the pauses between the clicks of the spyhole to rub the dust into the wounds.

This was all during a period when I was called for interrogation very infrequently. I was left alone in my almost windowless cell, walking and walking on my sore and inflamed feet. I remember the terrible resolve I needed to go on with this rather futile attempt at suicide. Inside, I guess I felt it was hopeless, but I was so desperate that I could think of nothing better, and I put all my concentration into this one attempt.

It took a week, but finally all my fingers were inflamed, my hands were full of pus, and somehow my entire nervous system was so sensitized that my skin hurt whenever I touched myself. I kept on dragging myself on those sore feet up and down and around that terrible cell, as if my body were a heavy bag that I was forced to carry around hell itself. My blood throbbed painfully through my infected fingers, and I hoped that this would be the beginning of the end.

However, it was not to be. After a long break, Kohoutek had me brought up to his office for interrogation and immediately saw my inflamed hands. When he asked what had happened, I explained that I was biting my nails, a nervous habit which he had already observed, and that the wounds had become infected. He accepted the explanation and had me brought to the prison doctor, who lanced and treated the wounds.

Although I had fed the wounds with dust at least twice a day, the treatment worked, and after ten days, my fingers were all but healed. I gave up. Recognizing how feeble my attempts were, I promised myself that I would resist and go on resisting as long as I could.

I do not know how many of my fellow prisoners tried to commit suicide, but there must have been others before me. When I came to jail, we had handkerchiefs. Later, those handkerchiefs were taken away and replaced by tiny pieces of cloth, because two people had tried to strangle themselves with them. I would have tried it myself, being so desperate, but by that time we had only those tiny squares.

I know that Slansky attempted suicide. He tried to split his skull on the concrete lavatory. He ran from the opposite corner of the cell and then threw himself in the air—head first—against the concrete. But he only bruised his head. Another time, he tried to commit suicide while being interrogated. When his interrogator turned around to speak with another officer, he tried to strangle himself with the cord of the telephone.

Under the conditions in our prison, suicide was impossible, especially for the more prominent prisoners who were under permanent surveillance. All of the fourteen defendants in my trial survived until the courtroom finale. The surveillance system was so watertight that not one case of successful suicide was registered among the prisoners whose names were known.

I have been asked why I did not attack my interrogator. He must have had a gun, and I was told that I could have tried to get hold of that gun and shoot myself or him, or be shot in the attempt. Such questions seem to be perfectly natural, but the idea never entered my mind while I was in prison. Not that I would have been afraid of the risk, for I had nothing to lose; it simply never entered my head. And I do not think any of my codefendants thought of it either. I may be wrong, but it seems to me that this kind of outburst was out of the realm of possibility for us prisoners. Nor did any of us, as far as I know, ever hit an interrogator. It was not a question of being afraid to do so; probably nobody ever thought of it.

The solitary confinement, the eternal walking, the poor food, and the lack of human contact crush the spirit of a prisoner to such an extent that no such attempts are possible. If anyone had advised me to use such means against my captors, I would have rejected the idea as absurd.

It would be wrong to assume that if a man is in a totally watertight prison or in a concentration camp such as the death-pens of the Nazis, he remains unchanged and behaves as he would under conditions of civilized freedom. Facing an over-whelming power, a human being uses his intellect to battle his jailers even though there is little chance of success. This applies particularly to intellectuals or to other people accustomed to fighting with means other than brute force. There might have been men so determined that they would prefer to be beaten to death than to give in, but I did not meet them, and I can relate only my own experience.

In World War II, during the terrible fighting on the eastern front, Germans captured Russian partisans, really brave people, and told their prisoners to dig their own graves. The prisoners had not spent months in solitary confinement and they knew that they would be shot, yet they dug their graves and then lined up to be executed. Maybe they just felt that it would be wisest to give up. Maybe they knew that the end was near and could not be avoided. Why be beaten up or hit before the inevitable bullet?

But there I was in my cell, walking on my inflamed feet, desperately tired and full of pain. In spite of all this, I clung with ferocity to my resistance and invented new pastimes to fight the crippling boredom.

I would pick a sheet of the party newspaper out from behind the toilet pipe, read the ads and the articles, and memorize them. I was particularly happy whenever sports events appeared in the paper, because memorizing the results was difficult and time-consuming. I remember that once I found a shred of paper with a crossword puzzle. I had never liked crossword puzzles, but this time I was enchanted to have one. It is difficult to solve a crossword puzzle even with a pencil, which I did not have. I had to memorize every line. It took me a few days to complete it, but I enjoyed every minute.

I used a similar method of memorizing when I was conducting my Marxist seminars and discussions with invisible students. It was in these seminars that, alone as I was, I defended my social and economic concepts, my Marxist interpretations of the past and the present, against the reality of which I had suddenly become a victim.

When the winds of history seem to blow in your sails, you do not doubt your righteousness, especially if you are successful. Not only individuals, but also whole nations embrace wrong doctrines and pernicious ideas and continue believing them even when the heavens rain flame and sulphur on their heads. Human beings—especially if they believe very firmly in an idea or an ideal—need time and palpable proof before they change their views.

Faced with the terrible reality of my imprisonment, and with so much time on my hands, I was constantly asking myself what had gone wrong, what was wrong, possibly what had been wrong all the time.

I had given my mind, my life, and all my energy to the party, and I had been happy when I was entrusted with running one of the most important departments in a small, land-locked country such as Czechoslovakia. I had let the Marxist theories and world view guide me at all times, but the humanist goal I had striven for had not been reached.

I knew that my comrades in the government had behaved correctly. We had done everything that followed from Marx's theory: we had expropriated the expropriators, we had made the working class the leaders of the country, we had replaced private ownership with societal ownership. Where was the society Marx promised?

What had gone wrong with the events in February of 1948, when the party had come to power? The cold war between the superpowers had brought about a split in our national unity. The Communists tended toward Moscow, the non-Communists toward Washington. The building of Socialism in Czechoslovakia necessitated that the country as a whole turn toward Moscow and that those who would not do so be eliminated. Even liberals like the late President Beneš and Masaryk had gone along with the Soviets; how could I, as a Communist, not go along?

We prided ourselves on the fact that the take-over in February was accomplished without bloodshed. Yet much cruelty and injustice had occurred. Non-Communists were fired from all important positions, and I, as the chairman of the Action Committee for the Ministry of Foreign Trade, had been instrumental in eliminating all exponents of the opposition. Farmers who did not want to join the collective farms had been imprisoned; owners of the means of production, even small-business men, had been persecuted, and many were thrown in jail for no real reason. Strict censorship was introduced, and, step by step, democratic freedom was abolished. Thousands who tried to leave the country were caught at the frontiers and imprisoned. Was this the kind of society I had dreamed of achieving through Communism?

In analyzing the Commune of Paris, Marx had advocated the dictatorship of the proletariat. We applied this philosophy. Why had it turned out this way?

I had always been able to persuade myself that throughout history, progress—as in the French Revolution, for example—had been accompanied by the suffering of innocents. I had also thought that it was not Marxism, not the system itself, but some unworthy people in it who were responsible for the evil that I witnessed. But I had to remember that Marx himself was not satisfied with accusing "some unworthy capitalists" for the evils of capitalism; he analyzed the system and came to the conclusion that the evils were inherent in the system as a whole.

These were frightening thoughts. What if the system I had believed in was wrong? What if Marxism, despite its humanistic aims, had all the inhumanity I witnessed inherent in it? In that case, I could not blame others, for I was to blame. I was responsible for everything that had happened—responsible for my own fate and that of my wife and son, responsible for all the injustices during the party take-over and for all the cruelty in our prisons. In that case, my whole life was a mistake.

I do not really remember when such thoughts and doubts arose for the first time. I always tried to avoid them and blamed myself for self-flagellation whenever I started thinking along those lines. I knew that I had to cling to my belief in Marxism as one would cling to a religion. My faith in it was my strength, the more so because I was faced with the question of my guilt or innocence for all that had happened. I felt it was an imperative for my survival.

But I became more and more curious as to whether what I had witnessed was a deviation from or a characteristic of Marxism. The desire to find the truth became stronger and stronger. The endless time I had to myself in prison created boredom, and boredom pushed me to think. Thinking was escape, even if I had to face results that would hurt me most deeply. Over a period of weeks, I tried to repudiate my doubts and persuade myself that Marx's philosophy was really a humanistic one. But as the time passed, I became more and more aware that Marx's basic assumptions were somehow wrong.

Marx's theories begin with the concepts that manual labor is the source of wealth and that the form of ownership of the means of production is the determining factor in a society. In addition, he says that the history of mankind is the history of class struggle, and consequently the world will change for the better if we change the form of ownership and make the working class the ruling class. As social development must move toward Socialism, it is our duty to use any means that would make such a historical necessity come into being.

This was the theory I began to question in fighting the pain and boredom in my cell. It was difficult at first: where does one start to question a theory that one has believed to be foolproof for so long? But once I allowed myself to begin, I found it easier and easier.

The key concept of Marxism was labor, meaning manual labor. This concept was also the point of departure for the classics of capitalism. What if Marx's concept of labor was wrong, what if it applied to nineteenth-century economy and society, and not to our times? If this were true, then the whole structure of Marx's political economics would break down: the proletariat would not be the creator of wealth or the leading stratum of society, and it would certainly not be the historical agent to change the world. Could this be the error that accounted for the antihumanism I was facing?

In questioning the theories of Marx, I was also forced to question my own beliefs and actions. I regarded myself as a humanist, but was that the way I had behaved? I thought of how I had been instrumental in introducing planning and how I had worked on our first Two-Year and Five-Year Plans, and I had to ask myself whether humanism and planning were compatible.

What had been the main concern for me and my fellow party members? It was how many tons of steel, coal, and grain, and how many shoes and other consumer goods, should be produced. We decided what should be produced and consumed, how much we should invest, and how much we should pay the workers. We were following Marx's program for Socialism, and man disappeared from our horizon: only commodities and their interrelationships occupied our minds.

We never asked anyone about what we were doing except the Politburo and the government. We had expropriated the owners of the means of production as Marx had planned, but had we not also expropriated the consumer, and was not the whole nation based on the idea of consumer rights? We had made the workers the ruling class, but their only function was to fulfill our target figures.

I was angry at myself for not having seen all this earlier. It was all so self-evident, and it had taken me such a long time in solitary confinement to be critical of what we, and I, had done.

The more I thought about the concept of labor as the source of wealth, the more I found that it was outdated. It may have been acceptable at the time of Adam Smith, but it was far less so at the time of Marx; in contemporary, mature economies, it was absolutely unacceptable.

Now, when practically all production was based on applied science, it was mental labor, not manual labor, that was the real source of wealth. The new social class of mental workers was both the cause and the consequence of applied science. Seen from this angle, even the most primitive work could be interpreted as the result of man's ability to think, and the prevailing level of thinking would be responsible for the level on which the economy developed. The more I considered this new source of wealth, the more I began to feel that it, and concepts related to it, should become essential elements of the science of economics.

With this discovery, I realized for the first time what a tremendous impact the conceptual prism through which we perceive our world has on us. I slowly changed this prism, and I found, suddenly, that what I had thought was absolute truth was actually an illusion, a fata morgana.

A person accepted certain fundamental assumptions and based a whole world view upon them. Once he had done this, he would further derive only those concepts, and thus would see only that which fit into the frame of his world view. As long as I believed in the historical mission of the proletariat, in the ultimate significance of the ownership of the means of production, and in historical determinism, as long as I saw only the inevitable doom of capitalism and the emergence and victory of Socialism, and as long as I felt that the result of our fight would be the creation of a humanistic world, I was able to condone any means of achieving this end: all was justified by the great cause for which we struggled.

This scientific objectivity that left no room for subjective values, and the absolute emphasis on the end without any concern for the means to that end, were the factors I found to be responsible for the inherent dehumanization of Marxism. Everything I witnessed in this prison had been justified in the name of the objective boon to mankind that would result from it, the triumph of Socialism.

I began to recall what I had seen in my country after the takeover in February, and also in the USSR during my visits. This time, however, my Socialist prism had been removed, and I saw things quite differently. I also began to reappraise Marxism as compared to the contemporary economics of capitalism. This time I saw in both of them a fetish of quantification, scientism, and objective laws. I realized that the foundations of Marxism and capitalism, despite their different rhetoric, were very similar.

From all of this followed a merciless logic: If I accepted Marx's humanistic point of departure and his challenge to move the world toward humanism, then I would have to give up and oppose his system of thought and conclusions. If I accepted Marxist theory, then I would have to give up his humanistic point of departure. I realized that I could not have it both ways.

Einstein once said that it is not so difficult to learn the new, the difficulty is in forgetting the old. I had my own vested interest in not seeing the new, but aside from this, transcending one's accepted views—suddenly seeing everything from a different angle and admitting one's mistakes—always involves fighting a tremendously powerful mental inertia. But for the pressure of boredom and endless time, I think that this inertia would have prevented my discovery of the new ways of thinking and my rejection of the old.

I cannot describe how painful this process was and how miserable it made me feel. I think that this conflict with Marxism, the loss of my faith, my religion—the loss of my entire world—made this the most tragic and desperate period in my life.

At this point I had lost everything. Imprisonment had taken away my freedom, my dignity, my wife, and my son. My own thinking had taken away my mission, and hence my belief and my hope. I had no prospects whatsoever, and I could not even escape through suicide. There was nothing to do but to continue living with the knowledge that everything I had believed in and hoped for was gone. It had all gone wrong; my whole life was senseless, and all that I had done had turned, not only against me, but also against my family and everyone else who had believed in me.

I was surrounded with absolute nothingness and absolute despair. Only one hope, one desire, was left: to die. To disappear and not to think.

Then one day, after forcing me to stand with my face to the wall for some twelve hours, Kohoutek suddenly got up and began to shout at me. He said that he and all his comrades in charge of my case had had enough of my stubborn resistance. If I wanted to keep on living, I would have to decide whether or not I was going to confess. If I chose not to, then I would be liquidated. With that, he had me led back to my cell.

The next day I was brought to the interrogation room again, and Kohoutek was especially hostile. He shouted at me at the top of his voice, demanding once again my immediate confession and threatening that I would be taken care of that very night in the cellar of the prison.

He got so worked up that I was really terrified. My hands trembled and I could hardly stand. I really wanted to confess then and there, but he kept up the insults, went on calling me names and flinging anti-Semitic abuse for so long that I got angry as well. This anger washed away my weakness and my willingness to give in.

That evening, he went on "interrogating" me through dinner, and I got nothing to eat. He repeated that traitors like me would not be fed by the toil of the working class and that my hours were numbered. As long as he kept on shouting, I took it as a bluff, but later, his voice dropped down to an icy coldness. When I continued to remain silent, he called a guard and, with a final threat, had me brought back to my cell.

I had just dropped onto my bed in an attempt to get some sleep when there was a knock on the cell door. A guard dragged me to my feet and blindfolded me with those goggles covered with black tape.

He took me out of the cell and turned me around in the corridor. We went on for a very great distance. I remember hearing our steps echoing through the quiet of the night until we stopped. I heard the key turning in the lock of another steel barrier, and the steps of another officer. Then they turned me around again and we went up a long flight of stairs; another turn, and we started descending.

It might have been the same staircase, or possibly it was another; I could not tell. I was staggering as if I were drunk; the guard was behind me, pushing me to the right or left as if I were a sheep being led to the slaughterhouse. We descended seven flights, and the echo changed. I thought that we must be in one of the corridors of the cellar. We walked endlessly, until finally I heard a door squeak and the guard pushed me into a room.

I tried to figure out what was going on around me. In the room where I was, there must have been an open door to the neighboring room. A man and a woman were there talking. Behind me stood a guard; I heard his feet moving on the concrete.

Minutes went by, and I was still standing in the middle of the room. The man behind me moved, and I suddenly realized that Kohoutek was carrying out his threat: I would be executed.

I heard a typewriter clacking terribly slowly. A phone rang. I thought I recognized the voice answering it: it seemed to be Kohoutek's. I heard him speak:

"He is already here. . . . No. Still the same. He did not confess. . . . Yes, Comrade. Everything is ready."

There was a pause, and then he said:

"Yes, exactly like Wednesday."

Another pause.

"I notified the comrades and they fully approve. . . . Good. I'll report as soon as we are done."

I was positive I would be executed within the next few minutes. I stood almost without moving and waited for the shot.

In my mind's eye, I saw a guard pointing the gun to the nape of my neck; I knew that was the way people were executed. I suddenly realized that I could see myself standing there and the guard in his gray military uniform with the Czechoslovak lion emblem on his armband and on his chest. As if I were weightless, I was floating up at the ceiling of the cellar, looking at myself—at "him"—without emotion. Wondering what I—he—was going to say, what his last words would be.

I should add that my first reaction to all this was a strange relief: now everything would end. I was observing myself and wondering how I would behave, or how I *should* behave. I started wondering if I should say anything, and if so, what my last words should be. Should I tell them that they were fascist bastards, or should I die with a revolutionary exclamation on my lips?

Then I thought of my son. If for nobody else's sake, I must die with one last loyal exclamation. If I acted offensively, he would not be permitted to study.

I could feel my bowels starting to move, but I controlled them; it was astonishingly easy. I was surprised that in these last seconds of mine, I was still vain. I thought of the impression I would make on the executioner. Maybe I would die as a hero, so that they—anybody—could say, "There died a real man."

I was all concentration and no feeling. I do not know how long I stood like this; maybe it was just one minute, maybe many minutes.

I suddenly realized that I was thinking of my mother-in-law. She had a favorite dress, red with white polka dots. She was very attractive and like a second mother to me. Fritzi used to say jokingly that I married her because of her mother.

I remembered that my mother-in-law had a dog named

Blackie. He was constantly the center of attention in her house. One day I brought my son—then three months old—to the house, and Ivan became the center of attention instead of the jealous dog. When my wife took the infant in her arms, Blackie jumped into his cradle to be in the limelight again. I have no idea why I remembered that silly episode at that particular moment. I smiled inwardly, and then the smile froze within my brain.

The phone rang.

Kohoutek answered. I was sure it was he, for I would have recognized his voice anywhere. He was a strong, bulky man, but he had the voice of a eunuch. Moreover, he had a lisp, and he always pronounced an *s* as *sh*.

"Yesh, Comrade. I followed your ordersh, Comrade. . . . Next Wenshday, Comrade . . . Undershtood, Comrade."

The door to the next room opened and someone said:

"Guard, take the prisoner back to his cell."

The guard grabbed my arm and led me back upstairs, through the endless corridors and into my cell.

I do not know how we arrived; I was ordered to go right to bed. I undressed and fell onto the mattress. I was still concentrating and absolutely under control. I observed, to my surprise, that I had behaved like a hero.

A few minutes later, my nerve broke and my whole body started shaking. I cried so loudly that the guard opened the door to find out what was happening. I could not check myself and went on crying and moaning. I was so depressed that I cried for hours, sleepless.

For the first time, I really understood that I was to die—next Wednesday I would be executed. I was already sentenced. It could even happen earlier, maybe tomorrow, maybe the next night. I would cease to exist. Suddenly, I wanted very much to live.

Previously, I had wanted to commit suicide. When I found out that my beliefs were wrong and that I would have to accept responsibility for all the evils I had witnessed, when all was lost, I longed for death.

But face to face with death, I was suddenly terrified. I tried to pull myself together, but it was impossible; I must have been suffering a complete nervous breakdown. The guard must have taken pity on me, because I did not have to report the whole night. I had the chance to sleep, but I was too excited, too desperate.

I was still reeling from the shock the next day. I was extremely tense, and whenever I heard the guard come near my cell, I started trembling. I thought they were coming for me, that this would be the end. I was terrified and then relieved, off and on all day: my terror mounted as the guard neared my cell; relief swept over me when he passed without stopping.

I tried to think, to invent games or something else to distract me, but I could not concentrate on anything any more. I was not even angry. Only the pain in my legs was real. It was the only thing that made me remember that I was still alive.

They did not call for me until the next Wednesday. They had to drag me out of my cell when the time came; I could not walk. My whole body was shaking uncontrollably. There was nothing left of the hero of the past week.

Once again, I stood blindfolded in the underground room, endlessly. Once again, I heard voices in the neighboring office, but this time, Kohoutek's was not among them.

I must have stood there for an hour, shaking and trembling. I remember that I suddenly started crying; tears were seeping from underneath the tight-fitting, tape-covered goggles. I felt their hot wetness running down my nose, dripping on the floor.

Then the office door opened and someone said, "Take him back to his cell."

When I was back in my cell, my blindfold removed, I started undressing slowly. Suddenly it occurred to me that it was all faked. They had arranged fake executions to frighten me, to break my resistance.

I was tense the next day, still anxious every time a guard came near my cell, but I started to wonder why I was so afraid of dying. After all, what kind of life was this? Wouldn't it be better to have it ended? There was no rational answer, but even so I wanted very much to live.

A week later, they took me to another "execution." I was naturally nervous, but not so excited as before. Once again they took me down those endless flights of stairs, through the corridor to the cellar, and there I stood blindfolded. Afterward, I was brought back to my cell. This time I knew that it was a fake.

These mock executions were just one more attempt to soften me up and extract a confession. I knew that my interrogator needed this confession for his own purposes. He needed it very badly, it seemed to me, just as badly as I needed to deny him this triumph.

Before the Fall

It is impossible to recollect that twilight life in detail. In the cell in which I was forced to walk around endlessly and without purpose, every minute resembled every other. The same pain and drudgery, the same infinite boredom. A routine of sameness. The days were getting shorter, rain was beating against the pane of the small window near the ceiling of my cell; I knew it was winter, yet, simultaneously, I had completely lost any concept of time. I was giving up, and I knew it.

It is also impossible to put the development of my thoughts in chronological order. I came to some conclusions and then forgot about them; I came to the same conclusions again, but from a different angle. It was actually a kind of chaos in thinking, jumping from theme to theme without any connection. Sometimes I would do nothing but think for a whole day, but it was a kind of circular thinking, very often thinking as an end in itself, just to escape reality. I do not even remember when I began to think of giving up my fight and confessing. I do remember that this idea played an ever-increasing role in my mind.

I felt that I was becoming schizophrenic, that there were two personalities inside me, and that they were fighting each other. One half of me argued that there was no meaning in fighting and resisting. This was a world without morals; why should I stick to the truth? Nothing would change if I confessed, nothing except the conditions under which I lived. They would change for the better. I knew I would be able to sit down again, and to read, and the idea of sitting, reading, and sleeping without being awakened every ten minutes was very appealing to me.

The other half argued with principles. I should not give up my ideals, it said. For a long time, Marxism gave powerful support to my resistance; to confess, to declare that I had betrayed my Marxist ideals, was too abhorrent.

Even when I came to the conclusion that all the evil that I saw was not a deviation from Marxism but an outgrowth of it, and when, in a long and indescribably painful process, I became critical of Marxism, I still found myself resisting. Listening to the moral side of me, I knew that once I confessed, I would be their tool. I would have lost myself completely.

These inner debates became more and more intense as time passed, to the point of hostility. At the same time, I became my own observer, so objective that I was even curious about how I would react; this experience was a very strange one and manifested itself in various ways.

As the objective side of me developed, I found myself observing not only my thoughts, but also my actions. I would watch myself as I cleaned the cell, made the bed, or even talked with Kohoutek. And, in observing my thoughts, I was able to see how that rational part of me, my pragmatic side, was slowly getting the upper hand.

In fact, the longer I stayed in prison, the more help my pragmatic side had in its fight. The pain in my legs, my aching body, the sleepless nights, the permanent hunger which not even meals could lessen, all contributed to weakening my organism, while the endless boredom and increasing hopelessness eroded my mental attitude. All of these elements became allies of my pragmatic half.

I cannot remember how often I decided to confess and give up all that I still treasured from my past. Had 1 been brought to Kohoutek in those moments of desperation, I would have confessed much sooner than I did. Sometimes I was almost willing to confess in Kohoutek's office, but, faced with his arrogance, his hostility, and his insults, I steeled myself, changed my mind, and shouted my innocence. Usually when I was brought to his office, he would scream at me, "Confess, you traitor!" This would anger me, and I would shout back, "I am innocent!"

Now he never let me stand by the window, and I could only see the outside in glimpses before being blindfolded. The fields near the airport were shrouded in mist, and one morning I saw them in the glorious white of freshly fallen snow. I still carry in my mind that wonderful impression of the first snow of the second winter of my incarceration.

Kohoutek made me stand in his office for endless hours, and he usually busied himself writing on his typewriter, letter by letter, while the machine ticked like an old clock. As I stood facing the wall, studying with dull and aching eyes the cracks in the paint and shifting my weight from one aching foot to the other, I was resisting with the last ounce of my strength. I was often tempted, when being led back to my cell, to ask the guard to take me back to Kohoutek's office so that I could tell him that I would sign whatever he wanted me to sign.

Back in my cell, one part of me would observe the other two parts of my personality battling it out over whether or not I should confess. On top of that, there emerged a fourth level which focused on thinking itself and avoided the conflict surrounding my confession.

The hours each day when I developed my thoughts gave me a feeling of great power. Having broken with the economic theories upon which I had previously based my faith, I began to work out a new economic theory, guided by the mistakes I had seen in both Marx and the classics of capitalism.

I began to think that my new economic theory would revolutionize the established way of thinking about economics and even the establishment itself. It is a difficult feeling to describe. It was not so much that I would publish the theory, but rather, that simply because I had changed my views and saw the world in a different light, the world itself had changed. Having lost all sense of the real world through my imprisonment, I did not find it so difficult, during those hours I spent lost in thought, to create my own world, and this brought me the feeling of absolute power and great strength.

Unfortunately, the feeling never lasted very long. Suddenly, I would become very much aware of the walls of my cell, my pain, and my exhaustion, and the reality of my imprisonment would come crashing down on me. Then I was not the creator of a new establishment, but the victim of the old one, helpless and miserable. And so here as well I was in conflict, vacillating between power and powerlessness, freedom and the walls of my cell. I was the center of the world, but a meaningless worm; the creator of a new, revolutionary economic theory, but a bankrupt Marxist.

And again, the objective, inscrutable part of me would watch the imprisoned Loebl pacing about his cell and alternating between being the master of the establishment and its victim, between the desire to confess and the will to stand fast. Most important, it saw how the wish to sit, to sleep, to smoke, and to read, the urgent need to overcome this deadening boredom and unbearable pain, became more and more difficult to control and to suppress.

At this point, the act of thinking meant far more to me than it ever had before. It was no longer just the pleasure of thinking, or thinking as an escape. Thinking became a means of self-realization, and it brought me a feeling of victory and strength. Yet I could think for only one or two hours, three at the most, before I would feel a vacuum. Then I could not formulate ideas any longer; it was as if I had lost my armor and became open to the attack of boredom.

Also around this time, my teeth started coming loose in my gums and I began to spit blood. They took me to the dentist, which I enjoyed immensely. I was handcuffed and blindfolded while I was in the dentist's chair, but at least I was sitting down.

I never saw the dentist, but he must have been a kind man, the only real human being I had met since I came to prison. He was very gentle and concerned about my health. He kept asking me whether or not he was hurting me and even patted my hand occasionally.

The second Christmas Eve I spent in prison was once more the only day in the year when I could eat my fill. We got large helpings of fried fish, potato salad, bread, and, on top of it all, a huge piece of cake. It was supposed to last for three days, but I gulped it down in one sitting. At least that one night I did not go hungry.

I remember sitting on the floor while I ate and hearing the click of the spyhole as the guard checked me—but he did not say anything. I stayed sitting on the floor, even after finishing the food, and the following night they let me sleep without the usual awakening every ten minutes.

They let me sit all day on Christmas and sleep for one more night. All in all, these comforts made a wonderful Christmas present.

But the biggest surprise was still to come. Two days after Christmas, when I was taken to the interrogator's office, Kohoutek gave me a sheet of paper and a pen. He said that I could write a letter to my wife and son.

My hand was trembling while I wrote. The paper was half the size of a normal sheet of paper, but I wrote as naturally as I could. I wrote a very optimistic letter and told them that I was feeling well. I assured them of how much I loved them, and I said I was looking forward to their reply. It is astonishing what banalities one writes when the heart is full and so many things must be left unsaid.

When I asked for an envelope, Kohoutek said that it would not be necessary. They would deliver the letter themselves. I was surprised that it took only a week for me to get a reply. I had been without contact with my family for thirteen months.

When they handed me the letter, I read it and reread it a hundred times, or so it seemed to me. I photographed it with my brain, since I would not be allowed to keep it and I wanted to memorize it. When I got back to my cell, I tried to repeat it word for word:

"It was the happiest day of my life when I got the message that you are alive. . . ."

My wife said that things were not bad for her and that she was confident that everything would turn out well in the end.

There was also a note from my son. Ivan was thirteen and a half now, and he was very proud of the fact that he could pronounce the letter R, which he had not been able to do when I left.

I was very happy that things were going well for them and that they were not suffering on my account. But very soon the happy feeling I had superimposed on my gray prison routine petered out and left me in an even deeper state of depression than before. After the elation of those marvelous three or four Christmas days, I sank into a deep despair.

Again and again, I saw myself trudging to and fro around the lavatory hole in a desperate effort to keep up my resistance. Although I had come to my new conclusion about Marxism, whenever Kohoutek accused me of not being a Marxist, I watched myself deny it again and again with desperate anger.

The interrogation sessions became more and more difficult as my doubts about my past beliefs increased. Kohoutek would curse me and continually accuse me of being a traitor, a saboteur, and a spy. He told me that I was a man who was anti-Marxist and antiparty, a Jewish louse who hid himself in the party, took on duties, made speeches, and gave lectures—all to hide the fact that I was really an enemy of the working class, of that great doctrine that was justifying the proletariat's world-wide march to Socialism.

It was impossible to tell him of my doubts and my inner split. I asserted again and again that I was a "true member of the church," because I knew that if I admitted that his charges were true on one point, my defenses would break down and there would be nothing left for me to do but to surrender.

As painful as it was and as much as I knew it was weakening my resistance, I could not help thinking. Once I had started to conceive of labor and economic activity as the function of man's intellectual ability, I found that all concepts that economists used, both Marxist and capitalist, required rethinking, and this was what I began to do. Without my even intending it, out of this critical approach new concepts emerged, through which I began to perceive a mature science of economics. And with this, the conflict between what I told Kohoutek I believed and what I really believed became greater and greater.

I was wavering between the two facets of my ego more strongly each day: one would use all rational arguments and try to persuade me to give in; the other, using the last ounces of my strength, supported me in further resistance.

I am now convinced that it was part of the interrogation method to allow the prisoner to persuade himself to give up. Nobody actually forced me to surrender; it would be wrong to say that they had. It was I who chose to do so. Of course, the choice was made under completely unnatural circumstances, but nevertheless, it was I who applied the final pressure and distortion on my personality.

The process is comparable to what happens to a hungry man who turns cannibal. It is a process of demoralization, and one gives in after having been demoralized. A typical sign of demoralization is that all one's bearings lose meaning, until they finally become nonsensical.

If I had a feeling of shame, it was very weak, and finally even that disappeared. One is ashamed only as long as one sticks to moral values, and I lost these values. I was not at all brainwashed; I was fully aware of what I was doing. But the strongest realization I had at the time was that moral and ethical values are only intellectual creations of men and human society.

During the process of demoralization, one begins to question whether the values by which one has lived, which were inherited over generations, have any meaning at all. It is like suddenly finding oneself on an island where there are no human beings.

One must create new values, for, in that kind of environment, the old values become an absurdity.

There was a time when I was prepared to die for my ideas, but now I had lost any sense at all of making a sacrifice for any standards. In such a situation, a human being is not immoral; he simply becomes amoral, beyond any human convention.

Walking in my cell, standing with my face to the wall during the interrogations, I felt my resistance growing weaker every day. I spent months, practically the whole winter, discussing what to do.

It was a vicious circle. I used all kinds of arguments to convince myself, even though I knew that that was exactly what they wanted me to do. And it was also clear to me that the moment I ended my suffering and gave in to them completely, I would become their tool.

I knew that one day I would have to give in; I had no hope of anything else. Very often I asked myself why I should wait any longer, and many times I actually decided to confess, but I always put it off, like someone postponing a dental appointment. Then I found that I was repeating the reasons why I should confess more and more often.

The pain and hopelessness were constant and difficult to bear, but they were external factors. The real reason I started leaning toward confession was that my spiritual resistance was dying. I was willing to pay any price for relief from that torture, even my own personality.

I tried to rationalize and called on thousands of excuses— that I would only be telling them something they wanted to hear, that I was only confessing nonsense—but I could not escape the fact that confession meant surrender, the denial of myself, and that I alone would have to bear the responsibility for this denial of my personality.

The longer I debated, the more complicated it all became. Confessing quickly for pragmatic reasons, such as under physical torture, would have been simple and easy. But as I walked up and down in my cell, running in that endless groove, I was incapable of deciding what to do. One minute I was pleading with myself not to be so stubborn; the next, I begged myself not to give in. I was split in half, and the half that favored confession was steadily gaining the upper hand. It got control of my mind and pushed the other ego aside. It was a struggle between two parts of my mind, and I felt helpless.

The part that favored confession won out.

The decision to confess made me very impatient: I wanted to get it over with. I paced the cell waiting to be taken to interrogation, preparing myself so that one second after I entered the room I could say, "I will confess." I saw the scene over and over again: it, too, became an obsession.

I knew that what I was going to do was wrong and that afterward I would be sorry and depressed. I even took full responsibility for it: I did not want or need any excuses. I pushed all worries aside and gave myself up completely to my need to confess. I felt an almost masochistic desire to give up, to humiliate myself, to stop being the person I had always been.

Whatever happened, I would confess. I swore I would.

The guard blindfolded me and led me down the corridor to Kohoutek's office. I repeated to myself the whole way, "Confess. Don't be stupid. Tell them what they want to hear. Whatever happens, confess."

When they took off the blindfold, I saw Kohoutek sitting at his desk, looking through some papers. He did not even bother to look up.

I tried to stand at attention.

"Mr. Interrogator, Prisoner 1473 reporting."

Kohoutek turned the page and went on reading without taking the slightest notice. I stood before him, a human wreck, full to bursting with my decision. But I did not say anything.

And suddenly, I heard a human wreck speaking:

"Mr. Interrogator, I want to confess my crimes."

A miracle must have happened. The man behind the desk who was looking into the paper suddenly turned his gaze at me, a smiling, happy, tender, and kind gaze. He got up slowly and put his arm around my shoulder.

"Take a chair, Loebl."

It was all like a dream. Blissfully, I sat down. Kohoutek offered me a cigarette and struck a match. I inhaled the smoke, and my head was whirling in a pleasant vertigo.

Through the clouds of smoke, I saw Kohoutek open the drawer of his desk and scrawl something on a blank piece of paper. After a minute or so, he handed me the sheet.

I have come to the conclusion that my confession will help the party rid itself of enemies like me that have crept into its rank and file. I have decided that from this time on, I will do all I can to undo the crimes I have already committed.

I confess out of my own free will, without any pressure whatsoever, that I have been an enemy of the party and of Socialism, and that in all the tasks the party gave me, I acted as a spy, a traitor, and a saboteur. As an agent of the Western imperialists, I did everything I could to destroy Socialism and re-establish capitalism in Czechoslovakia.

I will confess all my crimes. I will not spare myself or my accomplices. I will tell the truth, the whole truth, and nothing but the truth.

I was supposed to add in my own handwriting, "Read, understood, and signed," and then my signature. I read it, and then I read it again. I was innocent. I had always been a good member of the party, sacrificed my whole life for the party. I had always been an obedient soldier in the great army of Socialism. In the ranks of the party, I had striven to fulfill a great dream, not only for myself, but for all humanity as well.

No, I could not sign it.

I took his pen, and I wrote, "Read, understood, and signed, Eugen Loebl."

Kohoutek nodded understandingly, and, like an elderly doctor giving advice to his patient, he said, "From my own experience in these matters, Loebl, I can assure you that you will feel better now. You won't have to keep suffering under the burden of your guilt. You won't have to hide things any more. You will feel free to confess, and everything from now on will go smoothly. Go back to your cell and think about it."

I was still dazed when he asked me if I had any requests. I had some money left, and I asked him to buy me cheese, bread, and some cheap tobacco, and to let me have my pipe.

When I got back to my cell, it was all waiting for me, except that there were cigarettes instead of my pipe.

I bolted down the cheese and ate a pound of bread at one sitting. Since Christmas Eve, this was the first time I was not hungry.

On my bed, there was a copy of Sholokhov's *And Quiet Flows the Don,* in a Slovak translation by Zora Jesenska, a good friend of mine. I knew the book well, but I opened its pages with joy.

I remember the pleasure with which I asked the guard to light my cigarette. After smoking it, I could not resist, and I chain-smoked the rest of them. I felt no humiliation whatsoever; on the contrary, I thought that I had done the sensible thing. I did not blame myself for being weak, for giving in; I took it as some sort of a goal I had achieved, without any special value. I achieved something, and I received something. It is now, looking back after all these years, that I feel the dull ache down there, like a scar that has not completely healed.

The boon, the incredible pleasure of being permitted to sit and smoke, was such a terrible break—no, such a wonderful break—in the established pattern of prison life and resistance to the interrogators, that a resumption of that battle and another round of torture were something that I simply could not face. A few times, it came to my mind to revoke my confession, but immediately, I threw this notion overboard.

I confessed because I became demoralized. I knew that if I started another round, I would inevitably lose. Now I had the privileges of sitting, sleeping, reading, and smoking. I was afraid of losing those privileges, and I would not have minded getting life imprisonment as long as I did not have to walk again.

After the Fall

I sat and read all afternoon. After some hundred pages, to my surprise it was dinner time; it seemed as if only a few minutes had passed since lunch.

I sat with my legs crossed, taking long drags on my cigarette, reading, and eating. My legs still hurt, and even sitting was painful, but I felt so happy sitting there that every now and then I would get up and sit down again, just so I could enjoy the pleasure of sitting. When I went to bed that night, no one woke me up, and I slept uninterruptedly.

During the following days there were more interrogations. They lasted all morning and one or two hours in the afternoon, but my interrogators let me sit and smoke while I answered the questions.

Every day we constructed some new crime. It was really very easy: we simply took something that I had really done, and said that I did it to destroy Socialism or the party. For instance, when the German army occupied Czechoslovakia in 1939, I had fled to Poland and thence to Great Britain. Why had I not gone to the Soviet Union?

The real answer was that I had wanted to go to the Soviet Union, but the Soviets refused visas to any refugees. Only a few members of the party leadership were permitted to go to Moscow; the few refugees who were in eastern Poland when the Russians invaded it later in 1939, after the Russo-German Non-aggression Pact, had to spend a very long time in special camps.

The only visa I could get was from the British Committee for Refugees, and so I came to England more or less against my will.

Now, I confessed that I had refused to go to the Soviet Union because I had been an agent of the British secret service for a long time, and that I had channeled Czechoslovak refugees to Britain so that they could be recruited to become British spies.

My "espionage activities" were fabricated in the same way. I admitted knowing Godfrey Lias, the crack correspondent of the London *Times*. In my confession, I explained that Mr. Lias had told me he was a British agent, that I had invited him to my office in the ministry and given him all the information he wanted, and that Lias had even sent his secretary to see me so that she could take down my answers to some detailed questions he was interested in.

Now it is perfectly preposterous to believe that an intelligence agent disguised as a newspaper correspondent would simply shake hands with a high-ranking party member and admit to him that he was a spy. Or that the party member—even if he were willing to collaborate with such a spy—would take the man right to his office in a government building and give him, or his secretary, the requested information. Yet my interrogators asked me to confess that I had done exactly that, and I repeated it later at my trial. It was published in all the newspapers, and, however preposterous it was, people accepted it.

As I still had qualms about signing such confessions, I haggled and argued with Kohoutek and tried to give him the facts. But Kohoutek insisted on "clear-cut formulations."

"You admit to being a spy and a traitor, Loebl. The Czecho-slovak party and even the Soviet party are convinced that you are. Your duty to the party is to prove your guilt by giving us the facts. Naturally, Loebl, there were times when you gave out information that you were supposed to give out, and even times when you acted in the best interests of the country. But you did that only to conceal your real crimes. After all, Loebl, even a mass murderer doesn't kill everyone, and you can't expect to prove your innocence by talking of the people you did not 'kill.' "

Another time, the argument went as follows: "Suppose, Loebl, that an agent from a foreign power who wants to kill the President asks you where his home is. Now everyone knows where the President lives, but if you give this information to a foreign agent, you are acting in collusion with him and you are committing a crime."

When I still tried to object, Kohoutek told me: "The problem with you, Loebl, is that you still can't get used to the idea that you are a spy, a traitor, and a saboteur. You should repeat to yourself every day in your cell, 'I am a spy, a traitor, and a saboteur,' and you will see that, in time, you'll get accustomed to it." Just to be on the safe side, he had me repeat this statement at the beginning of every interrogation.

Some of the crimes I confessed to were absolutely absurd, even impossible. For instance, I admitted that I had made a very disadvantageous agreement with Israel—even though this agreement was not signed till six months after my imprisonment. I did not even know that it had been concluded. Nevertheless, I confessed that I had signed it.

After some initial resistance, I was ready to extrapolate a criminal act from anything. I felt no inhibitions; it became a kind of routine. Had Kohoutek asked me why I had had a son, I would have immediately confessed that I had had a son because I wanted to procreate a traitor to the party.

To say, "I am a spy," had no meaning any more. Yes, I was a spy, but so what? It did not matter. Had Kohoutek wanted me to confess that I was a murderer, I would not have denied it. Once you admit one crime, it all becomes a routine, ten crimes, thirty crimes, or a hundred crimes. With repetition, lying loses its sting.

I would like to repeat that I was not brainwashed. A forced confession is the result of a conflict between a particular man's values and external pressure. The kind of values does not make any difference—they might be political, religious, ethical, or just personal. There is a certain point at which the particular person will yield to the extreme external pressure and give up. *The stronger the resistance, the greater will be the effect of the capitulation.* The treatment I received is calculated expressly for the sort of person who resists fiercely. It goes to the very limits of his personality and breaks his resistance completely. Even so, I believe that there might be persons of extremely strong will or nerve or beliefs who cannot be broken.

My fellow defendant, London, and many others who had been in Nazi jails, said that what we had experienced was worse than what went on in the worst concentration camps or Gestapo torture chambers. The Nazis were more brutal, perhaps, but they always had to give up when the victim lost consciousness under torture. And after a certain amount of torture, a human being does not feel pain consciously. I was told that under such an excess of pain, human perception falters. The victim does not discern pain any more through his intellect; he feels pain just as an animal would.

The treatment we received contained a combination of brutality and scientific calculation. It was a very sophisticated method. They played with pain and with time. They knew how to focus the attention of a physically weakened prisoner, and, by gradual deprivation, by cutting off all sense perceptions and clues for orientation, they achieved a complete blockage of the prisoner's mind.

This combination of various psychological and physical methods might seem to be less brutal than the primitive Gestapo method, but it is definitely more painful and much more efficacious. Once a prisoner confessed as a result of this treatment, he could not retract his confession. The confession itself was a kind of breakdown; it was an expression of defeat, an acknowledgment of a situation that the prisoner did not have the strength to overcome. It was a psychological knockout that paralyzed all resistance, once and for all.

My confession did not mean that I had given up the fight; the fight continued on another plane. My "censor," the ethical part of my inner being, had been maimed through the treatment, and so my fight continued on a plane that was in itself immoral. My logic was that I had to be immoral because "they" were immoral; the contest continued, prisoner against interrogator, but the game and the rules were theirs. You may say that I simply became convinced that resistance was impossible, that suicide was out of the question, and that my ego was completely crushed. But the point is that I was conscious of it, that I was prepared to accept it.

A very strange and complex relationship developed between Kohoutek and me. Even in prison, under those terrible and unnatural circumstances, human beings do not behave like two-dimensional cartoons out of a play by Molière.

Once I confessed, I ceased to be Kohoutek's enemy. On the contrary, I became the source of his triumph, and he stopped caring whether I was a traitor or not. Now that he had succeeded, he had pleased his bosses and was certain of a promotion. He had wanted to sell me a confession, and I had bought it. Beyond this strange "business relationship," I was also another human being—or at least another "being," like an ape or a tiger whom an animal trainer has had to train for a certain act. After the animal has performed, and performed well, the trainer gets to like him.

Besides, even a secret-police interrogator is a human being. Kohoutek's life must have bored him, and his fellow secret-police men were probably not always the most advisable company. He was conscious that they would report on him. With a prisoner like me, he could be much more frank than with his comrades, who were subject to certain rules of behavior. After he had fulfilled his target figures—even the points in a confession are planned in a Socialist regime—he relaxed and talked to me as one human being to another.

For my part, Kohoutek was the only human being I had had real contact with for a very long time. I hated and despised him, but, at the same time, I was glad that in this artificial world in which I lived I could hear Kohoutek speak about the sexual problems he had with his wife, about his everyday worries. For me, these conversations were excursions into ordinary life, and that in itself was a great pleasure. My interrogations were sometimes quite enjoyable.

On the other hand, I was becoming more and more disturbed about how I was acting. They wanted me to reconstruct not only my own crimes, but also those of others: I was supposed to give them proof that certain accomplices were guilty of the same crimes that I was.

"After all," Kohoutek said, "sabotage like yours couldn't have been done by one man alone."

I tried to resist giving them that kind of "evidence," but I felt as if I were slipping into the mud a few more inches every day. I lacked any inner strength, any will power to resist. I knew what I was doing, but I felt about it the way one would feel about wearing a tie that does not fit with one's suit: it bothered me, but it did not affect my actions.

Kohoutek observed my hesitation and qualms with fatherly sympathy. He said that getting confessions out of me was like pulling teeth, but that I should relax and just get it over with; it was not really such a big deal.

To prove his point, he pulled a large file of photographs out of a drawer and showed them to me one by one.

"Don't think you are such a big shot, Loebl. You *were* our highest-ranking prisoner, but you aren't any more. We have so many deputy ministers, generals, and party secretaries now that there is a veritable flood of VIPs. So stop being so conceited; you aren't that important any more. You don't even have to be afraid that they will hang you. Compared to some of our prisoners, you aren't even that bad."

After a brief glance at all of the photographs, I watched Kohoutek arrange them on top of his desk, as a poker player might lay his winning cards on a table. There was a picture of Vlado Clementis, the Minister of Foreign Affairs; Gustav Husak, then commissioner of the government of Slovakia and since become first secretary of the Communist party and president of

Soviet-occupied Czechoslovakia; Marie Svermova, a member of the ruling Politburo at the time of my imprisonment; her brother, Karel Svab, Deputy Minister of the Interior; and Ota Sling, the party boss of the province of Moravia and Svermova's lover.

As new people were arrested, the teachers kept changing their plans for the trials, shuffling defendants and charges. Because of this, the nature of my crimes was changed from week to week. At first, I committed crimes because I was a Titoist agent; then I became a Zionist, a Slovak bourgeois nationalist, and, finally, a spy in the service of the Anglo-American imperialists.

The background for these criminal labels went something like this: I was a Titoist agent because of a five-year trade agreement I had negotiated with the Yugoslavs. I was a Slovak bourgeois nationalist as part of a group led by Clementis, who wanted to break up the unity of the Czech and Slovak peoples, under the orders of French, American, and British intelligence. Later on, the Zionist Loebl sold out Czechoslovakia and her economy to Israel, and finally, as an Anglo-American spy, I had attempted to drive the Czechoslovak Socialist Republic out of the Soviet embrace and into the imperialist camp.

During each leisurely five to six hours of interrogation, every day except Sunday, Kohoutek wrote some six to ten pages of confessions. After each confession, he compiled a short synopsis, which he called by its Russian name, *svodka,* in which he summed up what I had confessed on that day and how much progress he had made with me. These reports were sent to the teachers.

In a central office somewhere, the teachers were coordinating all the interrogations, collecting the confessions, comparing them, and issuing instructions for the following day. They might ask for more information on Minister X's ties to the Americans, or on General Y's sabotage of his Soviet army advisers. They wanted all the confessions to mesh and, at the same time, to contain every "crime" and detail.

I learned about this from my young Slovak interrogator. He was attached to me, because I was his first prominent prisoner.

He addressed me as if I were his father and asked my advice about his marriage problems and what kind of furniture he should put in his apartment.

As the days went by, I confessed to more and more with less and less resistance. Some of the charges and confessions were absolutely fantastic, and this gave me an idea of how to prove my innocence.

It occurred to me that by confessing the most outrageous crimes, I could render my confessions self-negating. I started toying with this possibility and slowly began to formulate my confessions so that they would be patently absurd. I found that as long as I began with the right introduction ("I confess as a sworn enemy of Socialism, the working class, and the Soviet Union, as an agent of Tito, the Anglo-American imperialists, and world Jewry that I . . .") the interrogator did not care what I admitted to having done.

I confessed that I had "smuggled" into the Czechoslovak Five-Year Plan the proviso that the entire foreign trade of the Czechoslovak Socialist Republic should be oriented fifty-five percent toward the West and only forty-five percent toward the Soviet Union. I was convinced that any man reading my confession would realize that this was nonsense. How could I be held responsible for a plan that was approved by the Politburo, the President, and the ministers, and finally passed into law by the whole Parliament?

Unfortunately, I did not realize that ordinary people do not know how a country is run. This is especially true in a Socialist country, where the press is so thoroughly muzzled that it cannot criticize or even inform.

Amateurish and poorly planned economic measures had been disrupting Czechoslovakia's economy to such an extent that there were severe disturbances and strikes. The people were angered by this, and the alleged sabotages and crimes attributed to us were a plausible explanation engineered by a faction of the party leadership that was determined to survive the crisis.

When it came to the trial, millions of people believed the

charges. They needed scapegoats for all the troubles that suddenly were defacing the structure of Socialism in Czechoslovakia.

In the early summer of 1952, I already knew that there would be a trial, and I wished it would be as soon as possible. I assumed that it would be public, so, in addition to making my confessions self-negating, I tried to formulate them in such a way that they would implicate foreign personalities in obvious and palpable untruths and thus force a public denial.

Weeks went by, and every day there were a few hours of interrogation in which I wrote out new confessions or expanded old ones. The charges against me were now changed more and more frequently. Kohoutek explained in detail why they were changed, who had been arrested when, and what the new defendants had been charged with. He became very talkative.

"Now prisoners like you, Loebl, committed your crimes for political reasons. The teachers have advised us not to use torture in such cases. You need time to think, to see clearly the crimes you have committed—to realize that denying the charges is senseless, and that, in the end, you will confess not from any outside pressure, but from the pressure of your own thinking. After you confess under these circumstances, you will stick to your confession, even at a public trial."

He stopped and looked at me almost kindly.

"You thought about it, Loebl, and you confessed—and I can tell you honestly that the teachers appreciate your confession, and it will show in your sentence. You don't have to worry about being hanged. We have so many big shots, and all of them have had more time to commit their crimes than you. You will be near the end of the list of defendants. I'm sure your sentence will be one of the lightest."

What Kohoutek was really saying was that my future would be bright as long as I stuck to my confession at the trial. It was all part of their method of assuring that, once a prisoner confessed, he did not retract his confession. But I did believe him when he said that I would not be executed.

Although my life was now physically easier than before my

confession, I still found it unbearable. I was not forced to walk any more, but I still kept on commuting endlessly down that one corridor, blindfolded, between my cell and Kohoutek's office. It seemed to me that any regular prison would be better than this terrible confinement. Every day I asked Kohoutek when my trial would be, and every day he told me that since so many big shots had been arrested, the trial had been postponed.

I was able to follow some of the new developments. They were now asking me what I knew about Dolansky and his antiparty and anti-Socialist activities. Dolansky was at that time minister of planning and a member of the Politburo and the Central Committee.

It seemed that every member of the government and the Politburo was on the teachers' list. They obviously wanted enough evidence to prove that anyone in a high position was a criminal, so that they could arrest him if they found it useful. Their dossier of all the leading politicians made them the real rulers of the country. They could produce a charge against anyone at any time. No doubt everyone in the ruling circles knew about their dossier, and no one dared to oppose them.

In the midst of this political upheaval, Kohoutek would often shift the interrogations to more everyday, personal levels. On one of these occasions, he told me that he was having trouble with his wife. She seemed to have political opinions different from his, and Kohoutek was on the verge of divorcing her. Another time, I learned from him that there was a special library in the prison composed of books confiscated from the prisoners. I asked Kohoutek if I could read some of them, and he granted my request.

I began to spend six to eight hours a day reading a fantastic variety of books—classics, political literature, poetry, and drama. This was a great help in fighting the monotony of my prison life. The more I read, however, the more I wanted to read Marx. I wanted to re-encounter my teacher, who, more than any other source, was responsible for how I had perceived my world. He was more than just a teacher, for my commitment to Marx was more than rational: his teachings were part of me, viscerally as well as intellectually. And so I asked Kohoutek for some of Marx's books.

Kohoutek said that prisoners were not allowed to read political literature. I insisted that, after all, Marx was a classic of Socialism; what could be subversive about a man in a Communist prison who has confessed to his mistakes and who tries to edify himself by reading the works of the very father of the movement? Kohoutek gave in, and the next day he brought me the first two volumes of *Das Kapital* and the rest of Marx's works, including essays and early writings.

I plunged into the books, gorging myself on Marx. I read quickly, but I stopped in places and went over some passages three or more times. And while I read, I thought constantly, debating with myself sentence by sentence. I was like a hungry man who eats so fast that he feels clogged up.

I was still impressed by Marx's commitment not only to interpret the world, but also to change it. I was deeply absorbed by his attempts to create a sociology that would change society and create a system for the service of humanity.

But as I read Marx from the new perspective I had created for myself, I became more and more convinced that in order to humanize the world, we must derive new theories and methods from the reality of the present rather than that of the past. With this idea as a starting point, my "dialogue" with Marx helped me to develop my own concepts, and I decided to write a book that would describe my new theory. I had neither paper nor pencil, but since I was in prison, I knew that even if I did have them, I would not dare to write down my thoughts. I would have to do it all from memory.

"Writing" this book became a most exciting experience. I began with my concept of labor and tried to interpret contemporary society from this angle. In doing so, I had to reformulate conventional Marxist and anti-Marxist concepts.

Having thought out what I estimated to be some twenty written pages, I began to go over them, polishing the sentences, deleting repetitions, and adding new thoughts. Very often I found that some of my conclusions were unacceptable, and I realized that I had made a mistake somewhere, that my thinking was not exact enough. I would have to think out everything again and look for the mistakes that I had made before I could continue. Because I was forced to work completely from memory, every time I discovered an inconsistency in my thinking, I had to go back to the beginning and repeat all my work until I found my error.

I soon found that in order to continue writing the book, I would have to research the work of non-Marxist economists, too. I also wanted to learn more about the scientific revolution in physics, particularly the work of Heisenberg, Einstein, and their contemporaries. I knew that my wife's parents could send me copies of all the books I needed, and I worked out a plan to force Kohoutek to allow them to do so.

I pretended to slip into a very deep depression and told Kohoutek that the novels I was reading were responsible for it. I told him that I wanted to read books on economics, philosophy, and natural science, and that my wife's parents, who were living in Austria, could send them to me through my wife if only I could have his permission to receive them. Kohoutek refused.

The next day I refused to answer any of his questions, and, after a short time in his office, I asked to be taken back to my cell. I figured that either they would begin to torture me again, and I would have to give up, or, in order to keep me healthy for the show trial, they would grant my request.

The next morning I was told that I could write my wife to send me the books, and I made a list of more than forty that I would need.

The first books came within a fortnight. I received books on economics and the history of philosophy and science and, later, at least ten textbooks written by professors in Austrian, German, and English universities. My cell began to fill with the works of Schumpeter, Marshall, Keynes, Hayek, Robinson, Kaldor, Einstein, Infeld, and others.

Reading as a political prisoner in a cell is very different from reading under normal conditions. There is no time pressure, no unread books waiting on one's shelves. As I had no paper, I had to memorize important passages, and I read almost every book at least twice. I had an average of six hours of undisturbed reading time each day, in which I could read 150 to 200 pages. I regard the reading I did during this period as my real university education, for I learned more from it than from all my years as a student—more, indeed, than from anything in my civilian life.

The General Secretary

The days were getting longer. I was halfway through my third year in prison, and there was no sign that my interrogation might end.

Then one day, when they took me to Kohoutek's office, there was only an aide waiting for me. He was very tense, and the whole atmosphere of the place had changed.

Suddenly, Kohoutek burst into the room. He was very excited, as if he had suddenly been promoted. He sat down behind his desk, pulled a folder out of one of the drawers, and opened it like a dramatic actor who is about to announce a new twist in the plot. When he spoke, it was slowly, as if his words had great historical importance:

"I appreciate the fact that you confessed, Loebl, but you still have not confessed your worst crime. You told us who helped you to commit your crimes, but you haven't told us the name of your real boss, the man behind all your crimes. No doubt you hoped that if you didn't mention his name, he would help you one day. Did you really think that we wouldn't find out in the end? Did you think perhaps that the teachers were not very good teachers? Well, Loebl?"

I did not know what he wanted. I told him that my confession had been complete, that I did not understand what else he wanted.

"Come now, Loebl. You know exactly who I mean. Remember how we broke down your lies and made you tell the truth? We can do it again if you don't tell us the truth this time."

I made an evasive answer.

"Stop worrying that your boss is still in power, Loebl. You needn't be afraid of his revenge. Maybe you think that he is also our boss and that we are trying to protect him. I don't blame you, but now is the time to speak out. Don't be afraid. Be a man, Loebl, and tell us everything you know."

I was more confused than ever. What did he want from me?

Kohoutek took a long look at me and said: "Tell us about your collaboration with the Anglo-American spy, Titoist agent, and Zionist pig, Rudolf Slansky."

Rudolf Slansky! He was the general secretary of the Communist party, the second most powerful man in the country; the party official, appointed for life, who controlled the whole party apparatus; the man who decided between life and death; the man who signed the orders that had put me and countless other party officials in prison. A close friend of Gottwald's. A trusted associate of Stalin's. I could not believe it!

"Well, Loebl, do you confess your relationship with this traitor, or do you deny it?"

I said I was too confused to answer and asked for one or two days in which to marshal my thoughts.

Kohoutek agreed, "in view of the importance of your expected evidence." Before I left, however, he said that I would not be permitted to deny anything. If I tried to do so, I knew what to expect: I would be set walking again, and the result would be a second breakdown. His tone was benign, almost fatherly. He hoped, he said, that I would do nothing rash or silly, and that I would not spoil my improved profile with him and the responsible comrades.

Back in my cell, I tried to understand what was happening. According to Kohoutek, Slansky was still in his office as the general secretary of the Communist party, but it was obviously only a matter of time before the teachers would have him imprisoned and tried.

I speculated that the teachers wanted various confessions implicating Slansky so that they could bring the charges to Gottwald. Gottwald, as president of the Republic, and, more importantly, as chairman of the Communist party, was the only man in the country who could approve Slansky's arrest.

But there was also the Constitution of the party to think of. The general secretary was elected by the party Congress, and at least the Politburo would have to agree to his arrest. My case was somewhat different; I was an underling who could be taken into custody on orders by Gottwald or Slansky. But with the general secretary, any move would have to be explained to members of the party.

Obviously the decision had already been made, but by whom? Certainly not by an unimportant official like Kohoutek. Not even the teachers were powerful enough to make that kind of decision. Yet I could not imagine that Gottwald had approved it—Slansky was his best friend. Besides, if Gottwald had wanted to get rid of Slansky, he could have arranged it easily without a trial, imprisonment, or any of the unsavory complications that would ensue. With Gottwald out of the game, there was only one authority that could have given the order: the Soviet leadership. And as the Soviet Union was a highly centralized state and the Soviet party was very disciplined, it was clear that a decision of such importance would have had to be approved by the very highest authority. No doubt, Stalin himself had made the decision.

But why would Stalin want Slansky in prison? Slansky was a devoted Stalinist, even more Stalinist than Gottwald. While Gottwald and our other leaders had their roots in Czech soil, Slansky was a typical apparatchik, whose only world was the party.

Then I realized that almost all of the imprisoned "big shots" were Jews. I recalled the anti-Semitic slurs of my Soviet interrogators, and I thought that maybe Slansky had become a victim of anti-Semitism in the party.

But I knew that anti-Semitism could be only part of the explanation. My real "crime," for instance, was an orientation toward the West; that I was Jewish was merely an accessory crime. Slansky had been oriented toward the Soviet Union all his life; what could the Soviet establishment gain by his indictment and imprisonment?

As concerned as I was about finding out the reasons for the General Secretary's arrest, I was even more concerned about what was going to happen to me. From Kohoutek's words, I realized that I would have to confess that I had been Slansky's accomplice, and I racked my brains thinking of what I could "confess."

My contact with Slansky had mainly been at receptions. In every Socialist country, the Communist party is the policy-making body and the members of the government are the executive branch. Being in charge of Czechoslovakia's foreign trade, I was part of this executive and had very little contact with the General Secretary of the party. I had merely talked to him a couple of times in his office about matters of no consequence, and I had never been invited to his home. There was nothing in any of our conversations that was even remotely suggestive or could be twisted into a crime.

On the other hand, after weeks of "privileges," I found myself dreading another onslaught of my former treatment.

But what should I confess? What could I confess? I knew I would sign whatever they wanted me to sign, but what could I invent?

As time went by, my excitement grew. I became more and more frightened. I could not sleep. I found myself concentrating on the single problem of what I could confess, searching for something, but nothing came to my mind.

I spent the whole night awake, staring at the peeling paint on the whitewashed ceiling and trying to find anything that would link me to my "accomplice," Rudolf Slansky, the General Secretary of the Communist party of Czechoslovakia. The morning came, and still I had thought of nothing.

Late that afternoon, it came to me. I was enormously proud. I felt like Newton when the apple fell from the tree and revealed to him the law of gravity. I thought that I had figured out a way to save both Slansky and myself.

Like all great discoveries, it was very simple: namely, that I would "confess" the discussions that had taken place between me and President Gottwald: I would tell them Gottwald's words and say that it was Slansky who had uttered them; I would take the opinions I knew Gottwald held and put them into Slansky's mouth. Neither Kohoutek nor the teachers would be able to detect my trick, and when my testimony reached Gottwald, as this time I was sure it would, he would have to recognize that the real accomplice in my "crimes" was himself.

No doubt the teachers had persuaded the President that I was a criminal by inventing stories about my contact with foreign diplomats and newsmen. Now, no doubt, he felt betrayed by someone he had depended upon and trusted. He had probably been misled about the "crimes" of everyone they had arrested. But with my charges against Slansky, he would know the truth.

I would make the President know that the charges against Slansky, his best friend and collaborator, were fabricated. From my cell in prison, I would reach out and let Gottwald understand how the teachers played their game.

I spent hours trying to recollect my conversations with Gottwald, trying to remember what he had said word for word. I was sure my tactic would work, and I was very pleased with myself. I was living in a strange elation, one of those "ups" in the periodic ups and downs every prisoner experiences. I was anxious to see my interrogator.

The next day, the guard came for me. As soon as I entered Kohoutek's office and the blindfold was removed, I spoke: "I will testify against Slansky."

Kohoutek beamed, picked up his phone and said, "Loebl *govorit*," the Russian for "Loebl talks."

We worked on the indictment for days. My formulations were often returned by the teachers with the comment that a particular statement had to be more specific. We wrote and rewrote the deposition until they approved it.

Kohoutek was very grateful for my cooperation. He was very proud to be a part of the group that was going to expose one of the highest officials in the country. No doubt the teachers were happy as well; by proving that even the General Secretary of the Communist party of Czechoslovakia was a traitor, they would be doing Socialism and the Soviet Union a great service.

It was later that I learned that by increasing their output of confessions and arrests, my interrogators—like all shock workers—were getting a higher bonus, and that by discovering ever bigger spies and traitors, they were assuring themselves promotions and raises in pay. No doubt his success in solving my case was one of the chief reasons for Kohoutek's advancement to the rank of major in the secret service.

Kohoutek told me that other prisoners were also confessing their collaboration with Slansky, and that it would be a few weeks before everything was completed and could be forwarded to Gottwald and the rest of the Politburo.

I did not mind waiting. If only Kohoutek knew what I knew; if only he could guess that by preparing the indictment against Slansky, he was preparing his own fall. A week before, things had seemed completely hopeless. Now, suddenly, everything—even that dull yellow door of my cell—seemed bright.

For the next few weeks I was not interrogated often. I was left alone to read and think sixteen hours a day. I made up a schedule for myself: which books to read, in what order, when to study, and what. I enjoyed this reading immensely. I spent a great deal of time thinking over what I read. The more I thought, the less time I had to worry about what it would be like to be free.

I was anxious to be free of cells, of interrogators, and of humiliation, but I also began to be afraid of freedom. Where would I go? My whole world had been shattered beyond all hope of repair, and I knew that it would be impossible to pick up my life where I had left off.

Throughout my life, I had acted only on my convictions; even the harsh measures I had taken when I was the chairman of the Action Committee of the ministry, even the wrongs I had committed, were products of my convictions. And now, while in prison, I had left those old convictions behind.

Outside of prison, I knew I would have to lie to remain free. Of course, I had to lie here in prison as well, but here, paradoxically, my lie was that I had been an enemy of Socialism, an enemy of the party. This was far easier than pretending that I was an ardent follower of ideas that I no longer believed in.

Besides, I was very tired. Frustrating as it was, maybe I was better off in prison. I had learned to comply with the routine, and it provided me with a haven where dreams were possible. According to the rules of logic, the opposite of imprisonment was freedom, but I suddenly recognized that it was not so. For me, to be out of prison meant only that I would be free to live in the shadow of what I had been. It would not be real life.

I was excited and worried, my moods changing instantaneously. One moment, I was voraciously devouring a classic or a book on economics. The next, I waited anxiously, trembling, for some word that my charges against Slansky had reached Gottwald. Finally, after I had been in complete solitude for weeks, the guard came. I was blindfolded and led down the corridor to Kohoutek's office.

As soon as they took off the blindfold, I could see that something had happened: Kohoutek's eyes were sparkling and he looked very self-confident. He got out of his chair, paced the office, and patted my shoulder.

"Well, Loebl, I have good news for you."

He could not have meant my release from prison. Good news for me would have meant very bad news for him.

"Gottwald has seen the charges against Slansky, Loebl, and the party leadership has already decided that Slansky is a traitor and has sentenced him. And you are to be congratulated, Loebl, because your charges were part of the indictment. What's the matter, Loebl? Are you feeling ill?"

I must have looked like I was about to faint. Kohoutek gave me a glass of water and called the doctor. I told him that I had not been feeling well for a few days; I could not tell him that it was his "good news" that had made me sick.

Kohoutek had me taken back to my cell, and a few minutes later, Dr. Josef Sommer, the prison doctor, came to see me. I had seen Sommer a few times before, and he seemed to me to be the cruelest and most ruthless man I had ever met. He was squat and bald, and he used to listen to the complaints of a prisoner and send him back to his cell as if the patient were an insect, not even important enough to be examined.

But this time, he was very attentive. He checked my heart, my pulse, and my breathing, and he prescribed pills, instructing the guard that I was to take them with my food. He was even polite and made an effort to be considerate. It was all a sign that my person and my testimony had become more significant in the calculations of those who ran this prison.

When he left, I was more desperate than ever. For weeks, I had lived in my delusion that my device would expose the fraud, and suddenly, my fraud was swept away by an even bigger one. I had thought that I would be helping Slansky and myself and that I would be able to expose the machinations of my tormentors. Now, I could see what a naïve fool I had been, what childish delusions I had had.

I could understand how Gottwald might have been tricked by false evidence into arresting me, but he must have known that the charges I made against Slansky were false. Why did he not defend his own policy?

The only plausible explanation was that he must have come to the conclusion that his own policy was untenable. Faced with developments of which I knew nothing, perhaps he was frightened of being branded as a Titoist, a deviationist, and a heretic himself.

Klement Gottwald, who had set out to build a new kind of Socialism, a Czechoslovak Socialism, obviously felt the need to streamline his policy with that of the Soviet Union.

I realized that my clever trick had backfired. My charge had returned with its full impact onto my own head and into Slansky's face: in declaring that his own words were treasonable, the President had proclaimed his realignment with the Soviet Union.

With my short-lived elation collapsing, I found myself in a depression that was so deep that I had occasional dizzy spells, and even Dr. Sommer's pills did not help me. The terrible scenario of which I myself had been a writer was taking shape before my eyes, and I was condemned to play a part in it whether I wished to or not. I was at the end of my rope; I did not have the strength to change or diminish my contribution. My only hope, my only justification for staying alive, was the prospect that one day I would be transferred to a normal prison. And there I would be free to commit suicide, if nothing else.

Drozd

Kohoutek became so busy with all the new cases that I found myself with a different interrogator. Lieutenant Josef Drozd was a good-looking man around forty, tall and well built, and he had a warm, shy smile. He spoke with the soft accent common to people who live along the Czech-Polish border.

In his own simple-minded, naïve way, Drozd was convinced that the Communist party was truly the representative of the working class. He was not much interested in politics, but he sensed instinctively the significance of his elevation to power. As the son of a miner, he had been recruited quite recently from the mines for the state security forces, and he liked his position even though he did not care for the job itself.

He did not actually interrogate me, but merely asked a few questions without attempting to work them into an indictment. It turned out that his only real job was to see me for an hour twice a day and talk to me. I guessed that after my last visit with the doctor, the interrogators were concerned about my depression. Talks with Drozd were supposed to keep it from getting any worse.

At that time, real black coffee was still a great luxury, but Drozd was able to get some and would share whatever he had with me. He was always very considerate, although he believed that all the charges against me were substantiated. He had read my confessions, but he had no idea what methods had been used to obtain them.

It was from Drozd that I learned of life on the "outside," what had been happening in Czechoslovakia since my imprisonment. He told me that the economic situation was very bad and that the people were dissatisfied. Electric power was being cut almost every day, and sometimes even twice a day. Trams did not run and food was scarce; there was not a plum or an apple in all of Prague, while fruits sent from Bulgaria were rotting in the freight cars. Ill-planned factories produced goods people would not buy. There were rumors that meat supplies for several months had rotted in the freezers because someone had given orders to cut the power for the weekend.

In glass-producing Czechoslovakia, there were suddenly no glasses to be had; people bought mustard in glass jars, threw the contents away, and used the jars for drinking. There were work stoppages in the sixty-thousand-man Svit (formerly Bata) shoe factory in Moravia, because the new management installed by the party did not know how to plan for a continuous supply of leather from overseas markets.

Before World War II, rich iron ore was brought by boat down the Oder River from capitalist Sweden. Now, Soviet ore of nowhere near as high quality was being hauled from the Ukrainian Donets Basin by rail over a distance of three thousand miles. The transport of these heavy loads over the country's weak railway lines was causing delays of up to five or six weeks. The sudden reorientation of the nation's industry had disrupted the economy. Butter, margarine, honey, and sometimes even bread disappeared. There were long lines even for such simple luxury goods as toilet paper.

The shortages had become so acute that all over the country workers were going on strike. The toilers struck against the Socialist establishment that was representing them; the members of the party revolted against the party machine. It became evident that an explanation must be found for the malfunctioning of the system the party had imposed upon the nation.

Culprits had to be found to serve as scapegoats. The entire machinery of the party, press, communications, and radio were

160

trying to uncover the culprits on whom the blame could be pinned, and special indoctrination classes and meetings were held to keep the public informed.

Drozd was convinced that the real cause was our sabotage. Now that our crimes had been discovered, people would trust the party again, and everything would improve. I expected him to hate me for causing so much misery, but he did not: he knew that I would be punished for what I had done, and he felt genuinely sorry for me. He said several times what a pity it was that such a clever and nice man like me was an enemy of his own people. He also said that maybe it was not too late yet, that the party was just and might yet give me another chance to use my talents, this time for the good of the working class.

Drozd did not like his new job. He said that he was ordered to join the security forces and that he would have preferred to remain a miner. Miners were much freer, did not have so much discipline in their work, and could make friends with whomever they liked. As a member of the state security forces, Drozd could now keep company only with other security agents. He could see his wife only once a week, and he was under strict orders not to tell her where he worked or what he did.

He told me many things I am sure I was not supposed to know. For instance, I learned that he also took care of Clementis and other prisoners. He told me about the Korean War and about the serious preparations taking place all over the country against what he was sure was going to be an American attack on Czechoslovakia. He was grateful to the Soviet Union for sending us military experts to organize our defense, especially against air attacks. They were building air-raid shelters all over the country.

As a party member—every member of the security forces was a party member—Drozd had to attend one party meeting a week. He did not tell me any special secrets, but we talked about what he had heard at those meetings. In time, I knew about as much of what was going on in the party as any state security agent knew, though Drozd was careful never to mention what the security forces themselves were doing.

At that time, every party member had to fulfill special reading assignments to maintain and elevate his educational level. The party authorities had set up a reading list, and every week one book had to be read and its contents and political import discussed at the meeting. Drozd found reading more difficult than work in the mines, and he never finished his reading assignment in time. He was delighted when I offered to read the books for him and prepare a short summary. Thanks to that arrangement, I got to read some very good books: an excellent translation of Leo and Aleksei Tolstoi's works, and others by Gorki, Pushkin, Lermontov, and even Dostoevski, who was at that time still blacklisted in the Soviet Union.

Occasionally we had to write indictments, and these took about four times as long as they had with Kohoutek. Drozd's grammar was atrocious, and his typing was even worse; it took him hours to type even a few pages.

After a few days, I insisted that he let me write the indictments myself. He read off a list of questions, and I wrote down my answers. Since he never changed anything I wrote, I started writing confessions so ridiculous that they were obviously self-negating. A few times I must have overdone it, because his superiors returned some of the confessions with orders to rewrite them.

In the strange state of depression I was in, concocting improbable indictments became an escape for a time. I knew that my situation was hopeless, but I still could not help trying to find some way out, however remote it seemed. I hoped that, by some miracle, these indictments would say what I had never had the chance to say myself, and that their absurdity would prove my innocence.

Kohoutek would sometimes drop into the office and watch Drozd question me. He seemed to be in charge now, and Drozd always spoke of him with the greatest respect.

One day they brought me to the office and only Kohoutek was there. He was sitting behind his desk, with the party newspaper, *Rudé Pravo,* propped up in front of him. He looked very pleased about what he was reading. When he noticed that I was standing before him, he looked up.

"Take a look at this, Loebl."

He showed me the front page of the paper. There was a large picture of Gottwald and Slansky shaking hands, and, above it, the headline, "Rudolf Slansky Celebrates Fiftieth Birthday."

The leader read: "Today President Gottwald and Prime Minister Zapotocky sent their warmest congratulations together with those of all Czechoslovak Communists to Deputy Prime Minister Rudolf Slansky on the occasion of his fiftieth birthday. In his message, President Gottwald emphasized the great contributions that this brave son of the working class has made to the Socialist revolution in our country. He also announced the publication of the collected writings and speeches of Rudolf Slansky in honor of the occasion, and awarded Slansky the Order of the Red Banner."

"Well, Loebl, what do you think of this?"

I did not understand. Only a few weeks before, Kohoutek had told me that the President had accepted the charges against Slansky, and that the General Secretary had already been denounced by the party. And here I was reading that he was being honored.

For an instant, I permitted myself a glimmer of hope that the President had read my deposition and discovered that I had used his own words in my testimony against Slansky. Perhaps Kohoutek had lied about what was going on, and all this nightmarish misunderstanding would dissolve into thin air.

"Just read carefully, Loebl. The article does not say 'General Secretary Slansky,' but *'Deputy Prime Minister* Slansky.' Don't you see? Everything is happening just as I told you it would. As the teachers say, things must always be done step by step. Now Slansky is only deputy prime minister, and everybody knows that he has made great mistakes. True, he has admitted these errors and criticized himself, but our working class is not to be fooled. You will see that the working people will very soon demand his arrest, and then we will act."

Kohoutek thought it was very clever of the President to honor Slansky and praise him while he had already sealed his fate. It was not a matter of morality; any lie that served a purpose seemed ethical to Kohoutek, and he saw nothing wrong with it.

I was struck dumb by so much duplicity. But, simultaneously, I was glad that I would not be alone any more. I confess I felt a certain satisfaction in knowing that others were now in the soup I was in. When Slansky had signed the warrant for my arrest and I had been imprisoned, I had felt terribly lonely. In those days, it seemed to me that all my friends were going to condemn me, just me and nobody else. Everyone would believe that I alone had done wrong. With Slansky's fall, my chances would improve. My chance for what, I did not know, but at least I would not be the archcriminal any more.

That does not mean that I did not feel a sense of solidarity with my fellow prisoners, even though they had been responsible for my fate; but in the strange state of mind of a prisoner, I could not help enjoying to a certain extent the fact that those who had doomed me were now also doomed. My reasons were very complex.

I had written a number of charges against various fellow prisoners, even though I was conscious of doing what my interrogators wanted me to do. I had given them the props to stage whatever they liked, but at that time, I attached no importance to my acts. In my state of mind and in the prison environment such values had no meaning. Besides, everybody had been sentenced in advance just as I had. It really made no difference.

Whenever I tried to say something positive about a fellow defendant, my words were twisted the other way around. Instead of helping the person, my attempts aroused suspicions that he was my accomplice and that I was trying to protect him and cover up. Paradoxically, it was better for my fellow defendants if I added to the charges against them.

Every day, I was shown charges that other prisoners had made against Slansky. There were two large files full of them even before his arrest. These charges were made up of some of the most fantastic lies I could imagine, and they were corroborated by one prisoner after another. With every corroboration, new "crimes" were added to the list. Everything Slansky had ever said or done, his whole life, became a crime.

There was a new element in the interrogations. Whenever I mentioned a name, Drozd would ask me whether that person was Jewish. When I mentioned a group of people, he only wrote down the names of the Jews. I asked him why he was using methods so similar to the ones the Nazis had used.

"This has nothing to do with anti-Semitism."

He said it as if he were telling me something of great wisdom.

"There are many Jews who are anti-Socialist, who have ties with their friends and relatives in the West, and who would like to make our country capitalist again. Personally, I've always liked Jews, but that's not the point. It is not that the party is against Jews; it is that the Jews are against the party. And so, to defend Socialism, the party must fight the Jews."

I must have looked unconvinced, because then he tried explaining it another way.

"Look, I like Yugoslavs. I spent three vacations in Yugoslavia, and I have a lot of friends there. But that doesn't mean that I shouldn't condemn the Yugoslavs for following the lead of the imperialist agent, Tito. It's a shame that we have to arrest so many Yugoslavs, and I am disappointed that they have turned their backs on Socialism, but the teachers say that it's only a matter of time before the Yugoslavs realize how much better off they would be if they supported the Soviet Union. The teachers say it's the same with the Jews: they are being misled by the Zionists and world Jewry into thinking that the party is their enemy. Nothing could be further from the truth. It is their Zionist leaders who are the real anti-Semites. And Jews everywhere will suffer until they realize that, and return to support the party that really represents their interests."

My third Christmas in solitary confinement passed, and there was still no sign of the trial. I was now permitted to write to my wife and son, but I could not see them. Their communications were the only link I had with the outside world, and they were hardly cheering.

My wife had been assigned to a textile factory outside Prague. She could not leave her place of work in search of another, and her wages were also prescribed by the Central Committee. Her work was hard; she developed a hernia and had to submit to an operation.

Ivan, now fourteen years old, was going to high school. He was told that he would only be able to stay there until his sixteenth birthday; after that, he could only stay if he got special permission, no matter how good his grades might be. It seemed unlikely that he would be granted that special permission.

He wrote me that he was interested in entomology. He had always loved insects; their secret world and strange way of life had fascinated him since his childhood. It grieved me that he would be assigned to some manual job instead of being able to explore his interest through education.

At least I could be proud of how my son was helping his mother. It was wonderful that he had turned out so well under such terribly demoralizing conditions.

I had already been in prison eight hundred days and did not have the slightest sign that it would ever end. Suspended between life and death as, in a way, I was, I wondered how it would end. How could it end? Would I be better off if I were sentenced?

I had some fantasies about miraculously leaving prison, but most of the time I could not help realizing the complete hopelessness of the situation. I expended a great deal of energy keeping myself from having a nervous breakdown. I often felt so close to it that I knew that if I got any more depressed or anxious, I would go over the edge. When I could not concentrate, the boredom was so intense that it was like physical pain.

On the other hand, when I was able to concentrate, I lived in the wonderful world of my own ideas. The "writing" of my book was going along very well; sometimes I could bring myself out of a depression by "opening" the book and "reading" from the memorized text. In these hours, I felt great satisfaction, and when

I succeeded in formulating new ideas and views, I felt a kind of happiness so pure and deep that it was unlike any feeling I had had while I was free. My feelings took me on an emotional roller-coaster ride—changing from the deepest of depressions to the heights of joy, sometimes from one second to another.

I often thought about what would have happened if I had confessed a year or so earlier than I did. I knew that the books and other privileges, if I had received them earlier, would have kept me from rethinking my convictions about Marxism and its principles, and I would never have come to think in my new frame of reference. I would most probably have remained convinced that all the evil I had witnessed and experienced was some kind of deviation from Marxism rather than part of its essence.

Then one day they told me that Slansky had been imprisoned. Despite the confessions of even his closest associates, the friends who had said that they were part of a conspiracy with him, he had denied everything.

I was told that I would have to confront him. I would have to be the one to tell him face to face what he was accused of. I would have to look him in the eye and call him a conspirator and a traitor to the party.

Confrontation

One morning they gave me two pages of excerpts from the things Gottwald had told me many, many eternities before—quotations from that confession of mine, which I had hoped would convince the President of Slansky's and my innocence. I tried to avoid the impending confrontation with Slansky, telling Kohoutek that I was getting dizzy again and that I was heading for a nervous breakdown. I said that others had confessed even more than I had; they had been arrested much later and had much more knowledge than I. Why couldn't they do it?

"It's the decision of the teachers," said Kohoutek. "It will only take five minutes, and the doctor will give you some tranquilizers."

I knew that I had been assigned as the tool that would help break Slansky's resistance. I tried to resist, but I did not have the strength any more.

I had never liked Slansky. The party line was his yardstick for judging everything, and the decisions of the Politburo, Gottwald's instructions in particular, were his bible. He always kept things well under control and never raised his voice; the only way to tell what was going on inside him was to look at his sharp, dark eyes.

He was tall, and he had reddish hair and a sensual mouth. His sharp features and penetrating eyes always gave me the feeling that he was ice-cold. People respected him, but they did not like him.

Slansky was completely devoted to Gottwald, and for years they had been the best of friends. In 1944, when the Slovaks attempted to revolt against the Germans, Gottwald had sent Slansky as his stand-in to the liberated part of Slovakia. Slansky dropped by parachute, together with Sverma, to create a foothold for the party in the first liberated territory in future Czechoslovakia.

During their retreat after the Germans recaptured the liberated territory, Sverma died in the snowstorms of the Carpathians, but Slansky was saved. His position as general secretary of the party made him second only to the President in the power structure of the country.

I reminded myself several times that Slansky was the one who had signed the order to have me arrested, and I tried to persuade myself that there was no reason why I should not repeat the charges to his face.

And yet I felt haunted by the idea of confronting Slansky. It was one thing to write confessions, and another thing to lie to a fellow prisoner face to face. The closer the confrontation with Slansky became, the more acutely I felt the terror of being a powerless puppet in the hands of my interrogators.

I knew that I did not have the courage to disobey the teachers. But I felt that I did not have the courage to lie to Slansky either. There had to be an answer to this dilemma, I thought, but I was at a loss to find it.

Kohoutek wrote a speech which I was to repeat when I confronted Slansky, and he had Drozd make me memorize it. For several days, we rehearsed the short speech in his office. The first part was an excerpt from the confession that was sent to Gottwald. Then the interrogator was supposed to say, "You have heard what Loebl says. Will you confess?"

If Slansky said yes, the confrontation would be over. If he denied it, I was to say, "I also denied everything for a long time, but then I found that there was no sense in denying and I confessed. You should do the same."

Drozd tested me, as though he were a director before a performance, to see that I knew all my lines. When I repeated everything I was supposed to say, he called Kohoutek to tell him that I knew my part by heart. Drozd listened to Kohoutek for a minute on the phone and then hung up. "Kohoutek says that you will confront Slansky tomorrow morning."

I felt dizzy and walked to my cell as if in a drunken stupor. I could not read, think, or sleep, and tranquilizers were no help. I was trembling nervously as I lay awake under the sharp light of the electric bulb, hoping that a miracle would save me. Then, in the middle of the night, I had an idea.

I remembered that I had once been telling jokes to a group of people at a reception at the Bulgarian embassy. A joke I had told about a Russian rabbi provoked so much laughter that Slansky, who was walking by, stopped and wanted to know what it was all about. I told him the joke, and Slansky thought it was funny. The key to the joke was the magic Yiddish word *oser,* which turned any sentence into its opposite. I suddenly realized that this word could get me out of my dilemma.

The next morning, I was left waiting in Drozd's office for about an hour. Finally my interrogator returned. "There are other witnesses now confronting Slansky with their confessions. You'll get your turn sometime in the afternoon."

I waited the whole morning, and finally I was blindfolded and led into another office. When the guard took off the blindfold, I saw that I was in a large room. In the corner opposite the door, I saw Doubek, the chief interrogator, sitting with a woman in uniform and a guard.

They placed me at a large table in the center of the room. I sat directly opposite Slansky, and I hardly recognized him. He must have been in prison for some time.

His face was pale, and the once penetrating eyes had the look of a hunted animal's. His hair was not just reddish, it was shining red, like a terrible wig. I realized that Slansky must have suffered more than I had. He must have thought a great deal about what he had done before he was arrested—how he had been betrayed by his best friends, how Gottwald, his lifelong comrade, had abandoned him, and how he himself had helped to create the situation that led to his downfall.

We were sitting opposite each other like two captured animals, two human wrecks. I had tears in my eyes, and I felt a tremendous sympathy and compassion for Slansky. He looked at me as if I was an enemy, as if I was one of the tormentors who would lie in his face and try to break his resistance. His eyes were filled with fear and hatred, as if to say, "Don't do it; it hurts." My whole body was trembling.

"Slansky, do you know this prisoner?"

Slansky nodded. "Yes, it's Eugen Loebl."

"And Loebl, do you know this prisoner?"

"Yes. It is Rudolf Slansky."

Slansky glared at me.

"Loebl, you have confessed that you were part of a criminal conspiracy which was led by Rudolf Slansky. Will you repeat your confession now?"

I said I would.

"Then go ahead."

I started my speech. And while I heard my voice trembling, I saw Slansky's eyes looking straight into mine as if he wanted to hypnotize me. "I committed a number of crimes as a member of the conspiracy led by Rudolf Slansky, *oser.*"

At the sound of that word, Slansky's expression suddenly changed. Never in my whole life have I seen a look as warm and grateful as the one he gave me then. His eyes embraced me.

I said one sentence after another and kept repeating *oser, oser, oser.* As we sat opposite each other at that table in prison, I realized that I felt like a human being again, and that through this communication, I was making another person feel human as well. If I did not have the courage to disobey, at least I could show that I was being forced to lie. And all this was done with the single, miraculous Yiddish word *oser*—addressed to the very man who had sent me to this horrible prison.

I finished my part, and Doubek said, "Slansky, you heard Loebl's confession. Will you confess?"

Slansky replied very resolutely, "I have confessed that I have made political mistakes, but I acted in good faith. I don't know anything about the conspiracy. Everything Loebl said is nonsense."

Doubek nodded at me to continue.

"I also denied, but finally I saw that it was useless to deny, and so I confessed. Do the same, *oser*."

We exchanged just one glance before I was led out of the room, and I felt that Slansky had become my brother. I was sure that he felt the same way about me.

The proof came at the trial, when he knew that he would die. After I finished my confession, Slansky asked the judge if he could be permitted to say a few words.

When the judge called him to the witness stand and the microphone, there was a sudden tension in the courtroom. None of the other defendants had requested to say anything that was not included in the trial's scenario. Everyone, including me, was curious about what Slansky would say.

"Your honor, I feel it is my duty to say that the acts Eugen Loebl confessed to were acts he committed on my orders. He had no choice but to obey. In view of this, I ask that he be regarded as innocent. I will take the full responsibility for his crimes."

At that time, we both knew that the sentences had been determined long before the trial. Slansky was obviously simply trying to thank me for my *osers*.

A day or two after the confrontation, Kohoutek called me into his office. "The teachers are satisfied with your part in confronting Slansky, but Doubek wants to know why you were always ending your sentences with *poser*."

I could barely keep from laughing. *Poser* is the Slovak word for shit. The fleeting moment of elation was a glimmer of light in my nebulous existence, which was rapidly turning for the worse.

I had begun to have attacks of vertigo during my interrogations, and one day I fainted. Drozd had me taken to the prison hospital, an office and several cells presided over by Dr. Sommer on the ground floor of the prison.

A Human Being

The doctor measured my blood pressure, took a blood test and urinalysis, and prescribed pills for me to take three times a day. Naturally, he did not tell me the diagnosis, but he made me stay in bed. I was not very worried; I hoped that I would get so sick that I would die.

There was another patient in the cell with me, with his right leg in a cast. I could not understand why they had put someone else in the same cell. Weren't my interrogators worried that I would betray a secret to him or try to smuggle out a message? I guessed that if he was in the same cell with me, he must be either an informer or a man sentenced to death.

As it turned out, my cellmate was a real spy. After all the interrogation, I was beginning to think that spies were only an invention of the teachers, but as the man told me about his work in great detail, I realized that "spies" really did exist.

When the war ended, he was twenty years old. He was a driver by profession, and he joined the party to seek a better job. He trained as a policeman, left for Sudetenland, and became an assistant policeman in a village from which the Sudeten Germans were being repatriated to Germany. The government decided at that time that these Germans would be treated the same way that the Germans had treated the Jews during the war.

As the living standard was extremely low in postwar Germany, the German population tried to hold on to their Czech homes as long as they could. With the arrogance of the former "supermen" gone, the German population saw itself at the mercy of the government and police authorities. They were harassed and subjected to the kind of humiliation that had been the lot of Czech and Slovak Jews when the Germans were in power.

My cellmate told me that he had made full use of his new power. When he saw a good-looking woman, he simply followed her to her apartment and made her submit to him. He added that he was well liked in spite of this, because he was generous after love-making; he gave the woman a pound of butter, some salami, or some cigarettes. When a woman refused, he put her on the list of people to be deported to Germany.

My cellmate used the border incidents as an opportunity to build himself an excellent record. He even caught some hapless Czech CIA agents who were being sent back to the Czechoslovak Republic from West Germany. He was in line for a promotion to lieutenant, but someone else got it and he felt hurt. In his simple mind, the idea arose that if his side would not give him a promotion, perhaps the other side would, and he decided to desert to Germany and join the CIA.

He told me that he was "not so stupid as to just walk across the border" and try to join his former enemies. He decided that he would leave in style, taking a rich dowry with him for his new bosses and showing his Czech superiors what an ingenious man they were losing.

He faked orders for a new car and a set of the most modern automatic weapons and then simply drove into Germany. He told me that the CIA was suspicious at first, but he must have given them valuable information, because, in time, he gained their confidence. He signed up for schooling with them in a villa near Regensburg, and, after reindoctrination, he got his first assignment. He was to return to Prague, contact certain addresses, and return to Germany with whatever information they gave him. One of his instructions was that, should he be captured, he was not to reveal the addresses in Prague under any circumstances for at least one week from his capture. This would give the contact persons a chance to go into hiding.

He started back for Czechoslovakia in a very confident mood, for he knew every foot of the frontier terrain and how the guards patrolled it and when. He set out one foggy night in autumn on a footpath that had been indicated to him as absolutely safe, but he had barely crossed the border when he was challenged by two guards with dogs. The guards seemed to be waiting for him.

He tried to make it back to Germany, but the dogs were at his heels. When he tried to shoot them, one of the guards fired at him, and the bullet shattered the bone in his thigh. After spending some time in the hospital where his surgery was performed, he was taken to the prison for interrogation. Since he had cigarettes and other privileges, there could be no doubt that he had confessed and given his interrogators all the information he had.

He was the first prisoner I had really talked to in prison. He was about twenty-five years old and very handsome, with an athletic body, blond hair, blue-gray eyes, and a winning smile. Although he had had almost no education, he had a great deal of common sense and was an excellent observer and storyteller. I did not tell him my name, but he guessed that I was one of the politicians who had been arrested recently; he knew the names of many of them and even mentioned hearing that "Loebl was in prison." I learned a good deal about the cold war from my cellmate, as it was a topic he seemed to be well informed on.

"I've seen the Americans with my own eyes. When the time comes, they will send their planes over Czechoslovakia, and there will be so many of them that you won't be able to see the sky."

He did not doubt for one second that the Americans would liberate all of Eastern Europe and defeat the Russians.

"You can't imagine how much money the Americans have put into their weapons."

He was all out for war, even if half of his country would be destroyed in the process. The philosophy of the push-button war had captured his imagination.

In his whole life, he had known nothing but ruthless dictatorship. In 1938, when he was a young boy, the Nazis occupied Czechoslovakia, and their values became his values; when the war ended, he used Nazi techniques, the only difference being that the Germans were now on the receiving end. He was aware of the cruelty of the Czechoslovakian State Security Police; he had used the same methods himself. And if the Americans conquered Czechoslovakia and opposed the present regime, as he assumed they would, he would happily use the same methods of brutality on his Czechoslovak captors as they had used on him.

Even at that time, I understood that although Hitler had died, his values were living on; while defeating Nazism and conquering the greatest evil of modern times, the victors had somehow become contaminated by it. They had done the world a great service by conquering one evil, but now they threatened to replace it with another.

My cellmate liked to talk, and I was happy to listen; after such a long time, it was a pleasure to have someone besides my interrogators to talk to me, and I enjoyed learning so many new facts—even if I had to pay for this privilege by listening to the repetition of some very primitive slogans. But I realized that he had not invented those slogans, he had heard them somewhere else; they were part of someone's propaganda.

He was afraid that he would be executed. He often told me that when a member of the security forces deserts, he cannot expect anything but the death sentence.

Bragging was an escape for him, a way of forgetting what was going to happen to him. One day he uncovered his unbandaged leg and asked me whether I liked it. I was never particularly interested in male legs, but I did not want to hurt his feelings and I told him that I thought it very handsome.

"When I went swimming in the pools in Prague, homosexuals used to flock around me; they simply loved my legs. I could have made a lot of dough that way, but I preferred women."

He paused and looked down at his legs.

"With legs like these, if worse comes to worse, I'll never be lost. I wonder if there is some plastic surgery that could remove the scars from the leg that got hurt?"

I tried to reassure him.

His outlook was very bright during the day, but sometimes at night, when he thought I was asleep, I could hear him crying.

One day he told me about how and why he had confessed.

"I would never have confessed; there is no way they could have forced me to tell them anything—I'm too strong for them," he said. "They would never have got it out of me. If the worst had come, I would have told them a lie.

"But I did tell them the truth, and do you know why? They showed me conclusive proof that they had had advance information about where I was to return over the border and at what time. Probably the CIA played the information into the hands of the Czechoslovak secret service to divert their attention from another spot on the border where an important spy would be sneaking in. They were using me as bait. The Americans were willing to sacrifice me, get me killed, just to get some of their spies into the country. And when our boys told me that the Americans somehow never trusted me properly, suddenly some of the things I heard in that school for spies seemed to me to be pretty phony. And so I thought that our boys were right and I told them everything. I offered to work for them again, against the Americans, but . . ."

He still hoped to find a way out, but in the back of his mind, he knew that his chances of resuming a spying career were nonexistent.

A few weeks later, when I got back to my own cell, Kohoutek asked me what I thought of my cellmate. I told him that I thought he was a nice boy, but rather confused—one of those people who could go one way or the other, depending on who was influencing him.

"Well, Loebl, I'm afraid he's beyond influencing now. He was executed last night," said Kohoutek dryly.

For days I thought about my naïve cellmate. During my life I have had the chance to speak to many great men, but none of them affected me the way that boy did.

Somehow, I saw in him the embodiment of the people who made this inhuman system work. He was important to me in another way as well: after so long in solitary confinement, I had become self-centered, and it was hard for me to think of the world's changing after I was forcibly cut off from it. My cellmate made it clear to me that the cold war was still raging, and that, if anything, it was becoming more intense.

It seemed to me that the cold war was the result of the decision by both superpowers to delineate their spheres of interest, and that the whole world had accepted the right of the two countries to protect those interests even in countries far from their borders. Czechoslovakia belonged in the Russian sphere of interest; the American government had agreed to that. Any human fly who would attempt to drift between those giants would be destroyed in the process. In an oblique way, what had happened to that poor, muddled boy was related to what had happened to me.

I was in this mood when Kohoutek had me brought to his office. He gestured at me to sit down in a chair facing him.

"It has been decided that the trial will take place toward the end of the year. In a few days, I will brief you on what will be expected from you, and then you can begin to write your testimony."

I told him I did not know what testimony would be needed.

"Your testimony will include all the questions that the prosecutor and the judge will ask you at the trial, as well as your answers."

I was not sure I understood what Kohoutek was saying.

"Do you mean that everything the judge and the prosecutor will say will be written down in advance?"

"This will be a political trial," Kohoutek replied. "It will be broadcast, filmed, and reported all over the world. There will be foreign reporters from the West. Everything, even the smallest details, must be rehearsed. The trial is a matter of state importance, and we have to make sure that it is at least as perfect as the Rajk trials in Budapest."

On Kohoutek's instructions, Dr. Sommer again took my blood pressure, X-rayed me, weighed me, and gave me a thorough checkup. Although I knew I was little more than skin and bones,

I was still surprised to see that the reading on the scale was barely a hundred and ten pounds; when I was arrested, I had weighed a hundred and seventy.

Sommer jotted my weight onto a chart in my file and then turned to the guard. "Put him on Diet #2. I'll clear it with Comrade Kohoutek."

The next morning at ten o'clock, the guard took me into the prison yard, and I was told that I would have an hour to walk around. While I was walking, another guard came over to me with a piece of buttered bread and some salami, which I ate.

When the hour of walking was over, they took me to Drozd's office for an hour of interrogation. Then I had lunch: some very good soup, a large helping of meat, two vegetables, and a dessert. After lunch, the guard came in and told me to take a nap.

At two o'clock, I went back for two more hours of interrogation, but this was interrupted by another guard who brought me more bread and salami. At about six o'clock, when my afternoon interrogation was over, I got a supper of meat, two vegetables, and a dessert of cheese.

This went on day after day. First they had planned my confession, and now they were planning my weight. I could even visualize the doctor setting his own target figures and doing whatever had to be done to make sure that the plan would be fulfilled.

I learned that the food I got was the same as that which the interrogators ate and on a par with the food served in the best restaurants in Prague. Some of my fellow defendants—the ones who had lost even more weight than I had—got even richer food. They were forced to drink cream three times a day and eat ham instead of salami, and they had beer with lunch and dinner. Diets were determined not according to rank, but according to weight loss.

Sometimes I was interrogated at night, but usually the interrogations amounted to only three or four hours during the day. It was still called interrogation, but it was very different from the sessions that I was used to.

Kohoutek called me into his office to brief me on my testimony. "The teachers are anxious to make sure that the defendants confess to certain particular charges and include all the necessary details in their confessions."

Here he stopped and took out of my file what must have been a list of my crimes.

"Your worst crime, Loebl, was that you tried to tie the Czechoslovak economy to the imperialist West in preparation for what you hoped would be a break from the Soviet Union. By making us dependent on trade with the West, you thought you could eliminate trade with other Socialist countries and restore capitalism to Czechoslovakia."

He paused and looked down the list.

"On top of that, you were a spy who gave valuable information to agents of the West, and a saboteur who tried his best to create economic problems in Czechoslovakia so as to discredit Socialism in the eyes of the working class, both of our country and of the world at large. You were also a Titoist agent who negotiated a treaty that was highly favorable to Yugoslavia and totally unfavorable to our country. Finally, you are a Jew who always did what was in the best interests of world Jewry and a supporter of Zionism, the bulwark of Anglo-American imperialism in the Near East."

He finished reading from the list, put it back in the file, closed it, and looked at me intently.

"Your job now, Loebl, will be to work out the exact wording of your testimony with your interrogator, Comrade Drozd. You will use your previous confessions as a basis for what you will say at the trial. Lieutenant Drozd will ask you the questions, and you will have to formulate good answers."

He ordered the guard to take me to Drozd's office. When I got there, I found Drozd pacing the room and looking very uneasy. He seemed to be uncomfortable in his role as assistant director of a play the whole world press was going to see.

"You know, Loebl, this business about writing the answers for a trial has to be done just right. The teachers are perfectionists, and if things aren't done exactly as they should be, they will get very angry. They've spent weeks briefing us on exactly how to do it. You know that Kohoutek and the others were present in Budapest, and they watched the preparations for the trial to learn how to proceed."

I remember the days of my youth, when the show trials started in Moscow for the founding fathers of the Soviet Revolution— among them, Bukharin and Radek. With the famous Vishinsky as prosecutor, all the defendants confessed and were sentenced to death or imprisonment. To the astonishment of an unbelieving world, not one of them protested. On the contrary, their closing speeches professed faith in the party, the Revolution, the Soviet fatherland, and the great cause of the working class. And like thousands of others all over the world, I believed in the genuineness of those trials; if I felt any doubts, I put them away.

One's perception of things is too often colored by wishful thinking, or by a bias. I had met former General Prosecutor Vishinsky, then in his function of minister of foreign affairs of the Soviet Union and delegate to the United Nations, and I had not felt that I was meeting a mass murderer. I was willing to accept only those facts that fit into the image of the world that I had created for myself.

I kept busy writing my testimony, but poor Drozd was not able to formulate the questions, let alone the answers.

By that time, I was ready to confess whatever I had to confess without offering the slightest resistance. Even in the midst of this tragedy, I could not help seeing that the situation had all the elements of a farce: where illiterate men like Drozd who could hardly spell were producing a show that would be seen by the whole world, and, at the same time, a helpless prisoner, sentenced even before his trial began, wrote all the questions that the prosecutors, attorneys, and judges would ask, as well as all the answers that he would give them.

Throughout the preparation for the trial, the teachers were careful to see that there were no contradictions among the statements of the various defendants. The confessions were to be like pieces in a giant jigsaw puzzle: they had to form a common picture which would demonstrate that the entire country, and all the important ministries and party organs, were in the hands of traitors, and that these traitors were disciplined members of a single well-organized conspiracy. Each of the defendants had his own special part in the larger scenario, assigned to him by its authors—the teachers.

Every day my questions and answers were being sent by Drozd to a coordinating center, and, after two or three days, they were returned to me with some comments. Depending on what the teachers needed, I had to add something or leave something out, or perhaps rewrite a passage. For weeks I was kept busy rewriting my testimony, even though the changes were sometimes minimal.

It took two months for my testimony to be finished and approved. The next step was to learn it by heart. Every day, I had to memorize a few pages of questions and answers. In a week or so, I knew it all by heart.

We rehearsed in Drozd's office. I had to stand in front of the desk, and Drozd, sitting behind it, asked me the questions. He read what the prosecutor, defender, and judge would say at the trial, and I had to answer from memory. I was not permitted to leave out or change a single word, not even the syntax. At the smallest mistake, Drozd repeated the question, and I had to repeat the answer until it was exactly the same as in the script.

After this rehearsal, I had to read the whole thing aloud, both questions and answers, so that I would remember it better. When Drozd saw that I knew everything by heart, he informed Kohoutek, who attended a rehearsal.

Both interrogators sat behind the desk, each with a copy of the script in his hands. Drozd asked the questions, and I answered them. After a short time, Kohoutek interrupted me.

"You seem to know all the answers, Loebl, but I am concerned about how you say them. You speak as if you didn't believe what you say. It is expected that you will answer with a firm voice. Your answers should sound convincing and decisive.

As you did confess of your own free will, we want everyone to see that this is so, and therefore, you should not hesitate when you answer. Your answers should sound the way you feel—that you wanted to confess, that you wanted to make up for the crimes you have committed."

I tried my best to play the role the way they wanted me to play it. Like an actor on stage, I was not concerned about whether it was the part of an honest man or a liar, a lover or a murderer, or how ridiculous the play itself was: I only wanted to do my best, play my part well, and be in harmony with the rest of the actors. I put out of my mind any thought that this trial showed the true morality of the regime and its real concept of justice.

In retrospect, what bothers me most is what I did not feel at that time—namely, that I no longer felt that I was a human being. Had I played the part out of fear or under pressure, had I hated it or been desperate at being forced into such a humiliating role, I would not feel the pain I feel now whenever I think of what happened. But at that time, I felt no shame or humiliation or hatred; I did not even make an internal protest about what was happening. It is this that still gives me a feeling of indescribable horror.

Yet I would like to stress again that I was not brainwashed. I knew exactly what I was doing. I thought, read, and learned more in those months than I had at the university. On the one hand, I read books on economics, physics, philosophy, and ethics; but on the other hand, every human value had been driven out of me, and I played my role without inhibitions.

It is frightening to think of how low I sank. It was as if I completely lost the human characteristics that are every man's legacy from the hundreds of generations that have gone before us.

Perhaps it would be better if I did not write about this, if I did not disclose how I feel today about what happened to me then. Perhaps it is just a kind of self-flagellation. But how could I write honestly if I lied about the worst part of the most horrifying experience of my life?

Let me emphasize that I am writing about my own experience. It happened to me, and I do not intend to generalize as to what others may have felt or to fit them into some kind of pigeonhole. I can only say that, for me, it was a nightmare.

Every person involved in the trial became an actor, a mere object in this devilish scenario. I remember that shortly before the trial, a young assistant prosecutor checked my confession and told me that I would have to reformulate my confessions concerning the Five-Year Plan.

"You can't take the blame for the clause that stated that fifty-five percent of the trade would be going to the West. The Five-Year Plan that contained the clause was approved by the entire government and became law. You'll have to rephrase what you are confessing. If the entire party leadership approved the plan, then the item cannot be evidence of your criminal activities."

I cannot explain why, but suddenly I got furious at him. Perhaps I did not want to be reminded that all my confessions were lies, not just this one. In my rage, I shouted at him that if he checked my other confessions, he would find that they all concerned acts approved by the party leadership. I told him that I would gladly retract the confession about the fifty-five percent of trade to the West, if simultaneously I could retract all my other confessions.

I remember that the young prosecutor went ashen: he could already see himself being charged with sabotage for encouraging prisoners to withdraw their confessions. He stuttered: "I think, Loebl, that you're basically right. Don't worry about that confession. I think it will be acceptable just the way it is."

Perhaps he realized at that moment, just as I did, how much even the prosecutors were victims of their own methods.

As the confessions grew longer and the time until the trial grew shorter, I sometimes played with the possibility of publicly denying my confession and revealing the whole truth. But very quickly I drove such thoughts from my mind. I felt as though I had lost the power to condemn what I was doing, that I had used up my moral strength, my dignity, and whatever values should have guided me. I wanted to confess, to do what they told me to do, and not to provoke any conflicts, internal or external.

Demoralized though I was, I continued to spend as much time as I could between interrogations "writing" my book. I was critical of both Marxist and capitalist economic theorists for having eliminated human values from their systems. They tried to be scientific, and, consequently, objective and value-neutral. I wanted very much to project human values and concepts into my new economic system, and, in doing so, to make economics an intellectual tool that could be instrumental in creating a humane orientation for our economy and for society as a whole.

While the work on my book and my feelings about confessing may seem to be contradictory, the product of a complete breakdown, I did not feel that way at the time. I actually lived in two worlds: there was the frightening world of the prison, real and yet Kafkaesque, and, simultaneously, the world of my thoughts. I created another reality in my cell in trying to learn from the past, from my mistakes and misconceptions. I wanted to use my newfound knowledge and ideas to contribute to a better world outside, even though I saw no possibility of communicating these ideas to anyone else.

This new world had a tangible reality for me. My endless hours of thinking were concerned with whether this or that view, this plan or another method I could devise, would actually have a humanistic impact on the world at large. It was as if the future of the world outside the prison walls really depended on the correctness of my analyses and formulations.

Although it is difficult to describe, when I think about it now, I can still feel as I did then. I remember that I once wrote my wife from prison and told her that the walls of my cell were covered with my views, as if they were a kind of wallpaper. Even the air of my cell was full of my thoughts and my notes, and it was all very real to me.

I was regularly moved from one cell to another, as part of the security routine. Each cell was the same as all the others, yet, when I moved, I felt like a stranger in a new and unfamiliar city, and I was very unhappy. I had to "furnish" my new cells; repeating what I had "written," making notes in the air, I had to put up my intellectual wallpaper before I felt comfortable in my new surroundings. It was usually two or three days before I really felt "at home."

There was a distinct separation between these two worlds as well. While playing my part for the show trial to come, I acted like a parrot or a tape recorder; the instant I was turned on, I made the required movements, the right sounds came out, and everyone was content. Returning from the world of my interrogators, I entered my own world where I was more at ease, and I resumed my thinking exactly where I had been interrupted for interrogation. In my cell, I was able to think, to read and criticize books, and to develop my own theories. I was alive again and deeply committed to a desire to live for my new ideals. I felt that I was a Titan—Atlas, who was compelled to support the heavens on his shoulders.

The prison, my interrogation, the testimony—all that became pseudoreality. To the world outside, I owed no allegiance; it had nothing to do with me. The only real world was the solitary confinement filled with thousands of thoughts. There I was a real human being, concerned with values, thinking of mankind, feeling a responsibility for the future of the world as I saw it.

Of course, this world of mine existed only as long as I embraced it. The very minute I stopped thinking, I became more aware than ever of where the *real* reality was. Nevertheless, in those moments I am describing, I felt free in a way I had never felt before.

Finally, the testimony was prepared. Drozd told me that all the other defendants knew their parts by heart. "Only Geminder has trouble," he said. "His Czech is so bad that he has trouble saying his lines."

So Geminder was in prison, too. With Slansky and Clementis, that made at least three other defendants. But who else? Even then, after almost three years in prison, I did not know the names of the other individuals who were allegedly part of my conspiracy.

Drozd continued. "The teachers have decided that the trial will take place toward the end of November."

Preview

A few weeks before the trial, I was taken to an office where I met a bald, very distinguished-looking gentleman accompanied by a young lady stenographer. Seated behind a desk, the man spoke in a professional, matter-of-fact way without looking at me. It was almost as if I were not really there.

"I am the chief justice of the panel of judges that will try you. I have come to acquaint you with the charges against you."

He quoted a few paragraphs in which I was charged with sabotage, espionage, and high treason.

"Were these confessions that I have here before me actually signed by you? Were they made freely, and are you prepared to repeat them in court?"

It did not enter my mind to reply in any other way but affirmatively.

The judge—his name was Jaroslav Novak—handed me a piece of paper.

"Sign this."

The document was dated November 24, 1949—almost three years earlier. The Office of the State Prosecutor confirmed that I was under arrest, and that the charges against me were high treason, espionage, and sabotage; also, I had the right to file an appeal against the order within twenty-four hours.

Chief Justice Novak asked me to sign the paper in October 1952, but this did not seem to disturb him at all. Nor did it disturb me; I signed it.

"Let me inform you that you have the right to a defense counsel," the judge went on.

"I don't want a defense counsel; I don't want to defend myself," I replied.

He looked at me sternly.

"The law says that you have to have a defense counsel. In the past, you disregarded the law; it's time you started obeying it."

To deny my guilt and declare that I had been forced to confess would have meant another ride through hell. As I had no intention of doing this, I did not see why I needed a lawyer. According to Drozd, I was to get a minimum of ten years and a maximum of fifteen years. What was the difference? I really did not care.

I shall never forget that strange, obstinate look on the face of Dr. Novak, who called himself chief justice and was to be the president of our court. Our show trial was to be the highlight of his professional career. He would be getting national, even worldwide, publicity. He could look forward to an excellent, well-paid position in the judicial setup that was rapidly developing to serve "class justice." The social role of lawyers was becoming superfluous in Czechoslovakia. Those who wanted to survive became pliable instruments of the new establishment and meted out seven or ten years to defendants whose class origins were not satisfactory.

As Judge Novak knew that all his questions and all our answers were on sheets before him, he must have known that the entire trial was a put-up job, a farce, and that we had learned both the questions and the answers by heart. From this, he must have been able to deduce that his function in the show trial was nothing but play-acting. The only difference between his role and mine was that he could read his part from the script in front of him, whereas my fellow defendants and I would have to recite our lines from memory. Even the sentencing, the principal function of the judge, was already decided, in an order from the Politburo.

Knowing all of this, Novak must have had some sense of the shamefulness of his role in the giant comedy that the trial was to be. I could not understand how he could remain so austere and impassive in the face of this awareness.

I had the same feeling when I thought about President Gottwald. How could he have acted as he had, condoning the arrest and imprisonment of so many of his comrades, without realizing what was going on?

Slansky and Gottwald might have decided to put me in prison in good faith. It was not impossible for a man in my position to be corrupt, and such misjudgment could have happened to any one of us. Even Gottwald's decision to imprison Slansky could have been based, at least theoretically, on proof. But when he got to read my confession, consisting of actions expressly approved by him, he must have known that it was a put-up job, just as Novak did. And if he listened to what happened at the trial, he would have to know that it was his policy that was on trial, not the defendants'. And not only Gottwald, but also all the members of the Politburo, the government, and the Central Committee—the entire establishment—must have known that it was a fake trial and that our confessions had been forced.

Gottwald could have been under pressure to condone this, although the pressure was possibly not direct. Perhaps the mere thought of opposing Stalin was so appalling that it was not necessary for Stalin to threaten him. He depended on Stalin a great deal, and had he not done what he had done, Gottwald would have had to face a lot of trouble; perhaps Gottwald himself would have been imprisoned. Such a fear would justify much that he had done.

But no one can deny his responsibility in agreeing to have eleven of his close collaborators executed, in agreeing to have the country he represented handed over to the Soviet Union, and in permitting the Soviet intelligence service to take over the country. As a politician, he was as much responsible for what he did as those so-called leaders of Czechoslovakia who cooperated with Hitler twenty years earlier and who were duly executed for treason after the liberation. Nobody loves traitors, and nobody has regrets when they die.

A few nights later I was dressed in my old civilian clothing and taken to another building. Drozd told me that I was supposed to meet my defense counsel.

The defense counsel was a short, well-dressed man with a completely expressionless face and a party pin on his lapel. As only the most trusted party member would be given a job like this, the pin struck me as unnecessary. He held a copy of my deposition in his hands.

"Have you confessed to all these crimes?" he asked.

I said that I had confessed to everything in my deposition, but that I did not know whether there were any crimes; that was for him to judge.

He looked at me as if he thought I was the greatest fool he had ever seen. He held in his hands a deposition full of confessed crimes, crimes so obvious that even a semiliterate person could recognize them as criminal and treasonable acts, and this former deputy minister, who had graduated from a university, did not seem to realize it. I had the impression that my lawyer thought that my confessions were real, though maybe slightly overstated, and that I was really a hardened criminal.

"Do you have anything to say in your defense?"

I told him that it was not my idea to have a defense counsel, that I did not want a lawyer, and that I did not want to be defended.

The whole conversation with my so-called defense counsel lasted less than ten minutes. Needless to say, the conversation took place in front of my interrogator, Drozd.

The exact date for the trial was set: November 24, 1952. It was precisely three years after my arrest.

Two or three days before the trial, Kohoutek took me to an office I had never seen before. Facing the door was a man behind a desk, a man wearing the uniform of a general. I had known the man for many years and I recognized him at once. His name was Karel Bacilek, and, at that time, he was minister of state security, a newly created position.

Before the war, he had been party secretary in Slovakia. A

former worker, he looked enough like Lenin to be his brother. I had always thought of him as a simple, honest, hard-working party functionary, and since that type of functionary was very poorly paid, I had often invited Bacilek to my home for dinner or taken him out to eat in a coffeehouse. I had even bought him cigarettes when he needed them, and I knew he had appreciated it.

He had escaped to Moscow during the war and, in 1944, parachuted into Slovakia to organize resistance against the Nazis. After the war, he became a member of the Parliament, and I often ran into him at various receptions or in trains. He had never played an important part in the government, but he was regarded as a hard-working, reliable apparatchik.

Now things were different. He had made a fantastic career for himself, and, as minister of state security, he was an influential member of the Politburo, a powerful and feared man.

Kohoutek told me to report.

"Mr. Minister, Prisoner 1473 reporting."

"This is the defendant Loebl," Kohoutek added.

Bacilek looked me over. He did not seem to recognize me.

"As you are no doubt aware, the crimes you have committed are the most terrible crimes anyone—especially a former member of the party—could commit. As you know, this is a political trial and has great political importance. Everything depends on whether you stick to your confession. Will you?"

It was clear to me that this was only a warning that, should I recant, I would be executed. Only if I stuck to my confession did I have a chance to survive. This threat was unnecessary; I would have confessed even if they told me that I would be sentenced to death. Bacilek just made it clear, once and for all, that the sentences were already written, even before I was tried.

Whether Bacilek knew of the "treatment" or not is not relevant. Although he was not very intelligent—he was a rather primitive man, in fact—he could not be unaware that the crimes we confessed to were, in reality, party policies approved by all the organs of the party and the state.

The preview was finished. A few more days and the trial would begin.

I finished my book well before the preview began and even devised a title for it: "Mental Work: The Real Source of the Wealth of Nations." But I was not at all happy to have finished. I had nothing to look forward to now, neither the pain nor the ecstasy of creating. To prolong my work, I went over each chapter, polishing some sentences and inventing chapter titles. I reorganized the whole structure of the book, reformulated some of my views, and did a lot of editing. I knew the whole book by heart and could go over any chapter at random as if I had a written manuscript before me.

Drozd told me that I would most probably be sent to a labor camp after sentencing. He advised me to work in the mines if I could and gave me all kinds of tips about mine work. He had obviously loved being a miner, and I began to look forward to it, having learned so much from his experience. He had told me that while he had worked in the mines, he had met many prisoners, and that miners and prisoners had been on friendly terms. It occurred to me that I might be able to put my book on paper and enlist the aid of civilian miners in trying to smuggle the manuscript out.

Opening Night

The night before the trial a guard brought me my civilian clothing and shoes. The belt and the shoelaces were missing, so that I could not use them to commit suicide. I went to bed apathetic, not at all excited. If anything, I was worried about whether I would remember all my lines. I was so caught up in the show that I wanted to play my part in exactly the right way.

It was still dark when the guard came and told me to get dressed. Then another guard came, cut my hair, and gave me a shave. An hour later, I was taken to the prison yard. The night was illuminated by huge lights. In the middle of the yard, there were buses surrounded by hundreds of guards in battle dress and carrying submachine guns.

My guards led me across the yard and up the steps of the first bus. Inside, there were four cells on each side of a narrow corridor. Every cell had a small door, and inside was a chair. There was just enough room to permit a prisoner to sit without moving.

One of the guards handcuffed me and locked the door from the outside; only then did I hear three more prisoners being loaded onto the bus. Those in the cells across the corridor must have got there before I came.

After an endless hour of waiting, the bus began to move. Then it stopped again. I heard a huge door being opened, and then the engine began to roar at normal speed. Outside, I could hear the sounds of metal treads on cobblestones; I guessed that our bus was being guarded by tanks.

I knew that the trial was to take place in Pankrac, an old prison built centuries before. The courtroom was in its courthouse annex, next to the Supreme Court.

Half an hour after the bus left Ruzyne, it stopped. Another heavy gate clanged, and we were inside Pankrac.

The bus door clicked open and then the doors of the cubicles, one by one. I counted; mine was the fifth.

The large, bleak courtyard of the medieval prison was dazzlingly lit by army searchlights which were reflected on the dewy cobblestones. There must have been a good hundred soldiers with submachine guns at the ready, and a dozen armored cars loomed in the rear near the gate; the place looked like a beleaguered fortress.

My first thought was, "What are they afraid of? Is the populace going to rise in revolt to liberate us—or do they believe the Americans are going to do it?" But when that first shock wore off and I stood in the glare of those lights, I suddenly realized that after three years in prison, I was now facing reality.

There, in Ruzyne prison, isolated from the outside world, I had been led to believe that I was the center of the world and that my prison life was the only true reality. In my isolation, I forgot completely about the difference between objective reality and the artifact, the artificial universe constructed in my immurement, by my jailers and myself. From that point of view, the coming trial would be just a welcome change in my status, and whatever testimony I gave would be pointless.

But in the glare of the searchlights that were cutting the misty predawn November morning, I suddenly realized that this would be a real trial, with a real public, and that I was a defendant in this trial.

Suddenly I realized anew the existence of all those values I had abrogated under the torment before my confession.

Up to that moment, I had been afraid that Slansky or one of

the other codefendants would deny my charges and expose me; I had only hoped that everyone would confess the way I did and that nobody would perform better than I. Being beyond morality myself, I wanted to evade a confrontation with people who had retained their morality.

But now, faced with the imminence of what was going to happen to me, I desperately wanted to be moral once more. I was aware that the Other One was not my real self. I condemned my past conduct and promised myself that, once in the dock, in the presence of the public and the press, I would expose everything; I would withdraw my confession and then maybe all the other defendants would withdraw theirs. In view of the publicity of the trial, not much could happen to me; the worst they could do was hang me.

At the same time, I felt in the depths of my being that I had neither the guts nor the strength to do anything. I had the moral strength to condemn myself, but not to do something about it. It was like being someone who was half awake, who felt that he should get up but did not have the strength to do so; instead he dreamed about what he would do if he did get up. This sense of weakness, of being paralyzed and knowing perfectly well how despicable my conduct was, was one of the worst experiences of my life.

Two guards took me to a cell two or three floors below ground. It was obviously a little-used cellar that was cut off from the other cells. There was no waterpipe or toilet. There was one iron bed, two chairs, a small table, and a large garbage can that I was supposed to use as a toilet. I was not left alone for a second. The guard stayed with me in the cell, but I was told not to speak to him unless I needed something.

Later that morning, they brought a wash basin and, in contrast to the meager furnishings, an excellent breakfast: real coffee with milk, ham, and buttered bread. It was the kind of breakfast that none of the members of the ruling working class could afford.

Dr. Sommer came to see me with his nurse, who was carrying a plate covered with different kinds of pills. Dr. Sommer gave me a thorough checkup and some tranquilizers, and we exchanged a few words. He was like a family doctor talking to a long-term patient.

The bell in the Pankrac tower tolled nine o'clock. A guard came for me, and we walked through a labyrinth of corridors. We were in the depths of the prison, and along the walls and ceiling I could see the pipes for central heating and water. There were two guards standing at every corner, making it impossible for anyone to come near us.

We walked up three flights of stairs and then down a long corridor, which was partitioned off into cubicles. Each of the cubicles had one chair for the prisoner and another for his guard. The partitions were in a row down one side of the hall so that the prisoners would have no chance to communicate with one another across the corridor.

Dr. Sommer and his nurse walked up and down the hall, distributing pills. High-ranking officers of the army and the secret police walked among the prisoners, accompanied by Kohoutek and the other interrogators; they stopped at each cubicle and exchanged a few friendly words with the accused. Several generals and colonels came to see me. They asked me how I felt and encouraged me not to be afraid of the sentence. They reminded me that the judgment of my party would be fair, and that I would be given every opportunity to make up for what I had done. They also said that, in any case, the party would take care of my family, and they offered me coffee, cigarettes, and soft drinks. It was as if I were surrounded by my best friends.

Suddenly there was a great commotion, and, one by one, we were ushered into the courtroom.

The Trial

The courtroom was a large hall with about three hundred seats. In front, there was a long bench for the judges; at the left, the bench for the prosecution; and at the right, the bench for the defense counsel. In front of the judges' bench, there were small tables for the court stenographers and many cameras and broadcasting equipment.

We defendants sat in the first three rows, framed on both sides by armed guards.

When I took my place in the dock, I saw my accomplices in the "conspiracy" for the first time; until that moment, I had not known who else would be on trial. I had known only that Slansky would be charged as the head of the conspiracy, and I had guessed that my old friend Clementis would be one of my codefendants.

Sitting next to Slansky was Josef Frank, the Deputy General Secretary of the party. He was Slansky's assistant and a fellow member of the Politburo. In spite of his German name, he was a Czech, originally a worker but a party functionary for many years.

During World War II, Frank had been in a Nazi concentration camp as one of a group of prisoners who took charge of assigning various jobs. It was a very important position, literally giving its holder power over life and death, since some work assignments were so taxing as to be equivalent to a death sentence. Frank used his position to assign light work to party members and sympathizers, to save their lives. For years, he was celebrated by the leadership as a hero who had saved countless Communists, but now, suddenly, he was charged with collaboration with the Nazis.

Next to Frank sat Bedrich Geminder, a very close and loyal friend of Gottwald's, and next to him Clementis. Farther down, I saw Karel Svab, the Deputy Minister of the Interior. On my bench, there was Ota Sling, the party Secretary for Moravia, a long-time party member who had fought in the Spanish Civil War, spent World War II in England, and would never have dreamed of opposing the party line.

André Simone, whom some called the "Czech Walter Lippmann," sat next to him. His articles were the mainstay of the foreign-news page of the official party journal, *Rudé Pravo*. During the war, Simone had lived in Mexico and spent several years in Paris. I hardly recognized him. He must have been about fifty, but he looked as if he were a hundred. His body was skin and bones, his face deathly pale.

Then came the Deputy Minister of Defense, Bedrich Reicin, a giant who was over six feet tall and looked even larger in contrast to the minuscule Simone. Reicin, who had fought in the Czechoslovak detachment in the Soviet Union and been decorated by the highest Soviet orders, was widely known as an agent for the Soviet army's secret service, and everybody in Prague was afraid of him.

On the other bench, I saw Dr. Otto Fischl, the Deputy Minister of Finance. Among other crimes, he was accused of permitting Jewish emigrants to Israel to take nearly all their possessions with them. Actually, Fischl had been disliked and feared because he was particularly severe with emigrants to Israel, in order to keep anyone from leaving who would not be loyal to the party. He was so zealous that he often went on inspection journeys to the borders to make sure that customs officials obeyed the rules.

Besides the economist Dr. Vavro Hajdu and the Deputy Minister of Foreign Affairs, Arthur London, there was also my friend and the Third Deputy Minister of Foreign Trade, Rudolf Margolius. After spending the war in a German concentration camp, he had emerged with great faith in the Soviet Union and the Communist party, and it was I myself who had advised the Minister of Foreign Trade to appoint him first his personal secretary, and not long afterward, deputy minister.

Altogether, there were fourteen of us, eleven of whom were Jews. Most of my fellow defendants had been party members much longer than I; many had spent their lifetimes in the service of the party, suffered imprisonment in capitalist prisons and concentration camps because of their devotion, and fought in the Spanish Civil War or alongside the Soviet Union in World War II.

The chief prosecutor and four assistant prosecutors took their places, followed by the four counselors for the defense. Then the president of the court, Dr. Novak, began the proceedings. Very formal, calm, and always dignified, he was the personification of objectivity, and he ran the show with a solemn voice.

"Will the citizen chief prosecutor read the indictment."

The chief prosecutor rose and solemnly began: "The accused Trotskyite, Titoist, Zionist, and bourgeois nationalist traitors created, in the service of the United States imperialists and under the direction of Western espionage agencies, an antistate, conspiratorial center designed to undermine the people's democratic regime, to frustrate the building of Socialism, to damage the national economy of the Republic, to carry out espionage activities, and generally to weaken the unity of the Czechoslovak people and the defensive capacity of the Republic.

"They did this to destroy the close alliance and undermine the friendship of the Czechoslovak people with the Soviet people, to liquidate the people's regime . . . undermine their close alliance, and liquidate the Socialist form of government in the Czechoslovak Republic. Their aim was to restore capitalism and to drag the Republic once again into the imperialist camp, while destroying its national sovereignty and independence."

The indictment made it clear that all of Czechoslovakia's economic and political difficulties were caused by a conspiracy of criminal individuals, coordinated by Slansky, who disguised themselves as party zealots and placed themselves in key positions from which, in close contact with one another, they would not only be able to turn Czechoslovakia toward the West, but also put the economy into such a chaotic state that the people would cease to believe in the leadership of the Communist party and the alliance with the Soviet Union.

After the indictment, Dr. Novak asked each of us whether we understood it, and whether we pleaded guilty or not.

Every one of the defendants was answering in the affirmative, and my turn was approaching. I wished terribly hard that I would be able to get up and say, "No."

But when my turn came and I was asked whether I confessed and admitted the crimes which were charged to me, I got up and said, "I do."

I cannot explain why I was unable to say no. I can only say that it was totally impossible. I just could not do it. The treatment had worked; it was foolproof. We played our parts in the scenario to the letter. We knew what we were doing, but we could not change it.

There were two sessions a day, morning and afternoon, during which they proceeded to question all the defendants in succession. Each night, we were transported back to Ruzyne prison in long black limousines, handcuffed and blindfolded.

My turn came on a Sunday. That particular morning, they took off my blindfold about a mile out of Ruzyne. It was a beautiful sunny day, and, as we drove through a park, I saw children being led by their parents on a Sunday outing.

In the courtroom, the prosecutor cross-examined me, and I confessed everything exactly as it had been written out in our scripts. The prosecutors, the counselors for the defense, and the judges had it all there in front of them—the questions I myself had conceived when I wrote my deposition with Drozd.

Everything went smoothly until one of the prosecutors asked a question before he was supposed to ask it; inadvertently, he had skipped a whole paragraph. I remember that I corrected his question and gave the correct answer. Practically no one noticed, but after the trial, Kohoutek told me that he was grateful that I had stuck to the deposition; he was furious with the prosecutor.

"How dare he make such a mistake! I assure you he will be severely reprimanded."

Kohoutek was very pleased with my performance. He said that I sounded absolutely convincing. But it must have been clear to everyone that the scenario of the trial was concocted; it ran so smoothly and interlocked so well. There was nothing unexpected or dramatic, such as would happen at a real trial. All of us defendants stated our crimes and our confessions in such exaggerated terms that it ought to have been obvious that this could not be our own wording.

The very smoothness of the judicial machinery ought to have alerted every thinking person to its phoniness, but I learned later that it did not. The many people who were listening to our voices on the radio, and the fifteen hundred or two thousand dignitaries, writers, newspapermen, and shock workers who were witnessing the trial were conditioned to accept our depositions and the entire trial as genuine.

True, there were only party members present, and even they had been carefully screened, but among them were French, Italian, and British Communist newspapermen who could not have been subjected to the various psychological pressures that Czechs and Slovaks were subjected to.

So the ghostly theater of the trial continued, with not only the spectators but also the nation and the whole Communist world as a terrible choir.

One day, the smoothly running clockwork of the trial had a ludicrous interruption, an event not foreseen in the script. The Moravian party Secretary, Ota Sling, had always been slightly obese, but during his time in prison, he had lost much more weight than he could gain back for public appearance. During his cross-examination, he had to hold his trousers up with one hand, as the defendants were not permitted to keep their shoelaces or belts.

The screenwriters of the trial had forgotten to reckon with the force of gravity. In the midst of the sordid, solemn ceremony, Sling, in the heat of his confession, suddenly gestured with both hands at the same time. His black trousers slipped to the floor and left him standing in his white underwear.

The judges, prosecutors, guards, defense counselors, and defendants—everyone—burst out laughing. With this laughter, something human crept into that court, something that had not been planned. And the mirth was so spontaneous that it was impossible even for Dr. Novak to stop it. The public and judiciary personnel were still laughing when we were taken back into the long corridor for the break between sessions.

Only Kohoutek and Sling's interrogator did not laugh; they accused Sling of doing it on purpose. I do not know whether Sling got a belt or whether they sewed his trousers to his shirt, but when the trial started again, Dr. Novak ignored the whole incident.

When I sat in that huge hall between my guards and saw one defendant after another come up to those microphones and accuse himself, and the others, of the vilest and most impossible crimes, I literally squirmed. How could they tell such foolish lies, so obviously untrue? And with such conviction! And how could they direct such ridiculously unlikely charges against me?

But when my turn came to confess, just like the others I could not escape that deep groove that had been dug into my psyche in the years of solitary confinement, and I, too, helplessly repeated the phrases engraved in my mind.

Drozd told me that he expected there would only be two or three death sentences, and that I, who had been imprisoned far earlier than anyone else, might expect a sentence of not more than ten or fifteen years. Nevertheless, this was not my reason for confessing at the trial. I knew that if I denied the charges, I would be sentenced to death, but what made me confess was not a fear of death, but a lack of strength and will power to act on my own.

I naturally cannot say what the motivations of the other defendants might have been, but all of us confessed exactly as we were told and taught to confess.

A hushed silence fell over the courtroom when the chief prosecutor began his final speech: "Our people's democratic court has never before dealt with a case involving criminals as base as those whom you see in the dock before you."

It was a very long speech, and he enumerated once again all the crimes and shameless confessions in which we boastfully had admitted our guilt. Finally he said:

"In the name of all of the Czech and Slovak people against whose freedom and happiness these criminals acted, in the name of peace, against which they shamelessly plotted, I demand the death sentence for all of the defendants."

He turned to the judges and raised his voice.

"Let your verdict become an iron fist that will crush these vermin without the slightest pity. Let your verdict be a fire that will burn out the roots of this shameful abscess of treason. Let your verdict be a bell ringing throughout our beautiful country for new victories on the march to the sunshine of Socialism. I demand the death sentence for all of the defendants!"

The audience answered with a standing ovation.

After a short plea from the defense counselors, we were taken back to our cells. I remember again my dual minds, one reacting to the events while the other, simultaneously, was merely speculative. During the trial, after three years of solitary confinement, I had been overwhelmed by the sudden contact with so many people. I had also been inquisitive; after my own experience, I wanted to see whether any of my fellow defendants had lost their souls the way I had. As the time passed and our sentencing drew closer, I felt my exhilaration and excitement petering out and exhaustion setting in, but this could also have been due to Dr. Sommer's medication.

On the last day of the trial, each of us had to make a final statement to the court. I cannot remember what the others said, but I do know that I spent the whole night thinking about how to phrase my own last statement; I was acting as if it might have some significance. I did not even think of denying what I had previously confessed; there was simply no escape from the steel ring to which I felt shackled.

In their last statements, all of my codefendants once again proclaimed their guilt and confessed their crimes. Several of them actually called for the supreme punishment and assured the court and the public that whatever punishment was meted out would be just, deserved, and exemplary. The party journalist, André Simone, even exclaimed in a ringing voice that there was not a gallows in the entire country high enough for a traitor of his caliber.

On November 27, 1952, the court pronounced sentence:

Eleven defendants were sentenced to death, three to life imprisonment.

London and Hajdu were sentenced to life, the court explained, because "the period of criminal activity was shorter than that of the others."

Loebl was sentenced to life because he was the first to be arrested, because he confessed spontaneously, and because his confession helped to unmask the conspiracy.

Besides sentencing me to life imprisonment, the court detailed the nature of my relationship with Slansky, trying to explain the inexplicable: how the General Secretary could approve my arrest even though he himself had been my boss and, at the same time, my accomplice in the conspiracy.

When, after the recess, the defense counselors flocked to our cells in the long corridor outside the courtroom, they advised us to waive the right to appeal and accept the sentence. Not one of the defendants appealed.

I must say again that in telling this story, I can only speak for myself. When I confessed, I knew exactly what part I was playing. What I said and what I did, I did and said because I did not have the strength for anything else; I was literally knocked out.

However, I have no intention of hiding behind the pressure I was exposed to. Deep inside me, I still have a feeling of guilt. I wish I could have been stronger and not given in. My denial could have influenced many of those who were listening and who were made to believe that the trial was a just one.

Eight Years

Immediately after the trial, I was taken back to Ruzyne. Still blindfolded, I was made to change my civilian dress for the tattered prison uniform. It was different from my first entry into Ruzyne: then, I had had hope; now I knew that I would die in those rags.

The Slovak wording of my sentence was even more brutal than the English. It translated not as "life sentence," but as "until the end of life."

As the shock and excitement of the trial wore off, I was indescribably sorry for those who were sentenced to death. Some of them had made charges against me—the charges that Kohoutek had read to me just after my arrest. But they must have been hard pressed to save their skins, and I felt their death had obliterated everything. They were all very dear to me.

I felt especially close to Vlado Clementis; he was the man who had brought me into the party many years ago. The more I thought of him, the more I envied him. Now, just after the trial, he might have been worse off than I, but very soon, in death, he would be beyond all this cruelty and barbarism. Perhaps a life sentence was worse than execution.

Eight years later, when I was released from prison, my first journey was to see his wife, Lida. I remembered her as the radiant Olympia in the National Opera's production of *The Tales of Hoffmann,* and she had seen me for the last time eleven years of prison before.

After we embraced, she said very drily that for some reason we had not had a chance to meet lately. And then she told me that inadvertently she had been the instrument of her husband's death.

Clementis had been attending a session of the United Nations as a representative of Czechoslovakia when Western intelligence found out that he was under suspicion and leaked the story to the press; several newspaper articles warned him not to return to Prague.

As the party leadership feared that Clementis might defect, President Gottwald invited Lida to the Hradcin palace, assured her of his complete confidence in Clementis, and suggested that she travel to New York and tell her husband that the President trusted him implicitly. So Lida flew to New York.

I seriously doubt that Clementis would have defected even without this cheap trick. Like me, he knew that he had done nothing wrong and that his place was among those who were building a new, progressive, and, as we then thought, better world in Czechoslovakia.

Soon after his return, Clementis had to resign from the ministry and was allotted a job in the State Bank. On an icy Sunday in January 1951, while walking his dog, Clementis was arrested; Lida was picked up a few days later.

Lida showed me a bundle of letters she had written to her husband from prison and, with them, Clementis's replies. In 1968, the letters were published in Prague under the title *Letters from Prison*.

The first was dated November 29, 1951, eleven months after Clementis was arrested; the last, December 2, 1952, a few hours before his execution.

Lida sat beside me as I read, drifting off into a world of her own. She was not allowed to tell her husband that she was in prison, and so she wrote him glowing letters telling him about whom she was meeting, asking his advice on new furniture, reporting the petty troubles everyone was having with housing—all as if these were her only concerns. While in prison, she contracted a lung disease, but she said she would have kept up the pretense indefinitely, so as not to worry her husband.

And then that fragile, sensitive woman with huge blue eyes told me that, on December 2, her interrogator called her to his office and told her that Clementis had been sentenced to death and wanted to see her. They brought in a hairdresser, gave her some make-up and a new dress, and took her to a cell divided by double iron gratings. Clementis was there already, waiting for her.

As he saw that he would not be able to embrace his wife one last time, he became furious and shouted abuse at the guards. He said that he would never have asked to see his wife had he known the conditions would be so inhumane, so humiliating.

He told her that in spite of everything, he had not given up his beliefs. He would die as a member of the party, a Communist, feeling that Socialism would prevail. He predicted that in ten or fifteen years, all of Europe would be Socialist, and that one day the record of what had been done to him would be discovered and he would receive full rehabilitation.

He was completely collected, not bitter or desperate at all. Only when she was about to leave, Lida saw a single tear running down his cheek.

When they returned Lida to her cell, she somehow could not believe—even after having seen him in death row—that his friends and associates, his lifelong comrades, would have him executed. As she could not sleep, she asked her warden to bring her some soap, a bucket, and a scrub brush, and spent the whole night feverishly scrubbing her cell.

In the morning, the chief warden had her brought to his office and informed her that the sentence had been carried out: her husband was dead. He assured her that throughout the proceedings Clementis had behaved manfully, that the execution had lasted only five minutes, and that it had not been painful. He also gave her two letters that Clementis had written during his last hours and two pipes that had belonged to him.

Lida showed me Clementis's last letters. In the first, addressed to his sister, he spoke of their dead mother and recalled the songs she used to sing to them. From the perspective of the world that their parents had lived in, he could see that great improvements had been made in the quality of life; he was certain that the direction was right and that the future was assured and bright. The most tragic moment of his life was ahead of him—soon he would have to say good-by to his wife.

There was a postscript: "I have just returned from seeing Lida. No words can express what I feel for her. And still I feel I have given her so much less than she has given me in these last hours."

Finally, Lida told me that the bodies were cremated after the execution. The ashes were put into a sack and taken by truck to be scattered in the countryside so that they could not be used as relics. But the roads were icy and the wheels of the truck were slipping, so the driver threw the ashes on the road. Later, he boasted in a tavern that at last those traitors had been put to some good use.

Clementis is dead; he cannot tell us anything, and I can only speak from conjecture. But it seems to me that a martyr can never be absolutely frank with himself, because to be a martyr a person must create for himself the image of a martyr. Many people who know that they are to die protect themselves that way; the American John Brown did it, and so did our own Jan Hus before he was burned at the stake in Constance in 1415. I remember that when I was in prison and felt very desperate, I was always comforted by the thought that it was better to be the victim than to be one of those who made me a victim; that I was among the "just" and that they were among the "unjust" people. They were the villains, and, from the perspective of history at least, I was in an infinitely better position.

One requires such an image for self-preservation; it is one of the imperatives for the survival of one's personality. It is a great temptation to stick to it and not admit any of the human weaknesses that go with man no matter what situation he is in.

One does not think in terms of an image consciously. It is, rather, in the back of one's mind; one just lives in it. In prison, there is no reality, only pseudoreality; prisoners create their own world and become the center of it. And the isolation in a prison is so complete that prisoners do not need to be made to believe in this or that situation; they make themselves believe it.

After the sentencing, I felt as if the waters had closed over my head. Every day, I was more convinced that I would end my life in solitary confinement. Time after time, I asked the guard to take me to my interrogator, but days passed and nobody came.

I was taken for a walk for fifteen minutes every day except Saturdays and Sundays. The special food was canceled, and once again I lived on the normal, very poor prison rations.

After two weeks, a guard took me to see Drozd. Probably Drozd had me brought to his office out of pity. There was no interrogation; he just wanted to talk to me.

"I was on vacation. So was Kohoutek; he was just promoted to major."

A decent if simple-minded man, Drozd looked unhappy.

"I never expected those sentences; none of us did."

He was particularly sad about Clementis, whom he had also interrogated. Drozd had obviously become very fond of him.

"All of them requested clemency, but it was refused. The sentence was carried out, and all eleven have been executed." He spread his fingers out on the desk in front of him and looked down at them. "I will get another assignment soon, and someone else will take over. It is very possible that you will be interrogated in connection with other cases."

I asked him what would happen to me.

"You will be taken for a walk every day. You can have books to read, but it has not been decided how long you will have to stay in solitary confinement. That kind of decision has to be made by the highest authorities, and I have no idea how long it will take."

A month, a year, several years?

"Anything is possible; I can't give you any guarantee."

I asked for a piece of paper to write to my wife and son and permission to see them. He granted my request.

I sat down at a small table in my cell and began to write. I looked at the piece of paper and tried to pour all my feelings into that one letter. I was shaking with dry sobs. That letter might look pathetic and theatrical in retrospect, but at the moment it was real, and very practical.

I asked my wife and son not to think of me; life was over, and from now on they should think only of themselves. I suggested that my wife should sue me for divorce. Under the circumstances, there was little doubt that it would be granted. This divorce would be useful not only to her, but also to our son, Ivan, who would thus be freed from a very burdensome connection with his past. I also advised her that it might be useful for Ivan to assume another name.

I paused and stared at that little piece of paper. It was difficult to compress all the feelings exploding inside me onto the tiny page. I wrote that they should apply for permission to see me. A visit might give us a chance to discuss all these matters. And, lastly, I confided that putting my feelings down on paper had made me somehow more aware than ever of what had happened to me and what I could look forward to.

Later that day, Drozd read the letter. When he finished, there were tears in his eyes. A few days later, he informed me that he had received a letter from my wife requesting permission to visit me. Since he censored my mail, he read all the letters she sent.

"You are lucky to have such a devoted wife and son; very few prisoners have such loyal families. London's wife, a relative of a member of the Politburo in France, wrote a letter to the president of the court declaring that she realized what a monster her husband was and demanding the maximum penalty. A son of another codefendant of yours wrote a letter to the president demanding death for his treacherous father and publicly disavowing any connection between his father and himself. Frejka's wife refused to see her husband before his execution."

I knew Frejka's wife well. She was devoted to him and had abandoned her career on the stage to become his wife. I found it strange that she should behave like that.

Drozd also told me of the mass meetings that had taken place in Prague. In the Ministry of Foreign Trade there had been a protest meeting against the leniency of my sentence. A resolution demanding that I should be executed with the others was passed.

Drozd was very depressed, and I had the feeling that he was beginning to doubt Kohoutek and the teachers. He said he would be the happiest man in the world if he could be released from the security forces and return to the life of an ordinary miner. He wanted nothing more to do with politics.

Two weeks later, I was told that my wife and son had got permission to see me. I was permitted to put on my civilian jacket for the occasion, and a guard took me to one of those empty offices that were reserved for special purposes.

A few minutes later, my wife and son appeared. They stood before me, suddenly there, alive and smiling, wonderful. I remember sitting stiffly, getting up, and trying to smile. I was bursting with joy, and scared at the same time; they probably felt the same. My son had been twelve when I saw him last, and now he was past fifteen. He had changed quite a bit. I looked at Fritzi and saw that her hair had turned gray and her beautiful black eyes were surrounded by wrinkles.

I could see in their eyes how shocked they were when they saw me. Despite all the fattening up, I must have looked terrible. Later, I learned that my wife had written her mother about our meeting: "Eugen is an old, broken man." I was forty-five years old.

They brought me a small parcel—some fruit, ham, salami, and cheese. As Fritzi untied the string, I saw that her hands were trembling. I learned that she had been imprisoned in Ruzyne for six months, and seeing it again was an unbearable shock for her.

I was not permitted to take any food with me to my cell, but I could eat as much as I wanted while I was there with them. Fritzi had also brought two cigars, and I smoked one for the first time in years.

Eating, lighting cigars—all these small actions helped to bridge the gap that I felt between us. We also tried hard to bridge it with courageous small talk, while Drozd sat in the corner reading a newspaper and pretending not to hear us.

In spite of our efforts, I felt the growing tension between my wife and me. I saw her hesitate. She turned to Ivan.

"Tell your father," she said.

Maybe if our son would speak about the possibility of a divorce, I would not think that it was she who really wanted it.

Ivan said that they had discussed my letter and my suggestion of a divorce, with each other and then with some friends and my sister. Everyone agreed that it would indeed be better for both of them if Fritzi and I divorced and they assumed another name. If she tried to get a job and said that she was my wife, the personnel department of even the smallest state corporation would be afraid of complications. And there were zealots constantly pestering both her and my son as well.

My wife believed that an assumed name would bring her some relief, but she immediately added that the divorce would of course be only a formality. She would never desert me. She would stay with me, visit me, write me, and wait for me.

We agreed on a divorce. Their visit lasted less than an hour, but after more than three years apart, even so short a time proved to be too long. I could not say what I was thinking, and neither could they. We all felt the widening gap of those three years and the terrible events that had happened in them.

There were to be more visits. By the next one, Drozd was gone and a new interrogator was sitting in his chair and listening to our conversation. When my wife asked him whether she would be allowed to visit me if she got a divorce, he told her that this was against regulations. Only a relation could visit a prisoner, and a divorced wife was not allowed to see her former husband.

"Then I won't ask for a divorce," she said, and my son agreed.

They were prepared to risk all the consequences of being associated with me, as long as they could see me from time to time. I was and I still am deeply grateful, not only for their love and devotion, but also for their courage. Every visit left me more convinced that their lives might be even more desperate than my own. My wife was hounded from job to job and from apartment to apartment; my son was barred from further study and was facing employment as a factory hand.

It was their example that helped me out of the deep depression I fell into after their first visit. Their courage, their daring, their kindness, their love for me—all this helped me overcome my despair.

Inside the prison walls, nothing changed, but outside, history was marching on. Stalin died, and with him perished Lavrenti Beria, his henchman and dreaded minister of security. Excerpts from Khrushchev's revealing speech before the Central Committee of the Communist party of the Soviet Union after Stalin's death were being spoonfed to meetings of Communists in Czechoslovakia. No one was permitted to read the entire speech, and written copies of it were numbered and had to be returned to the Central Committee from each party cell.

While attending Stalin's funeral in Moscow, President Gottwald caught a strange disease from which he later died, in spite of the efforts of the best Soviet specialists, who were rushed to Prague. His body was mummified and carried, exposed under a glass cover, in a giant funeral procession through the streets of Prague, to be exhibited in a shrine overlooking the city.

Nikita Khrushchev flew to Belgrade to embrace and publicly apologize to that archtraitor and watchdog of the Western imperialists, Yugoslavia's Marshal Tito.

At that time, I was in a concentration camp in a uranium mine in central Bohemia. Most of the prisoners who worked in the mines had contact with the civilian miners, and so newspapers were smuggled into the camp. Besides that, every evening, the camp radio broadcast official news at seven o'clock. In spite of my imprisonment, I kept informed about what was happening "on the outside."

It was from the radio that I learned that both of my interrogators, Kohoutek and Doubek, were arrested and charged with using unlawful means during their interrogations. Shortly afterward, two members of the chief prosecutor's staff had me brought to their office and read me parts of Kohoutek's and Doubek's confessions. Very much in the style of the confessions they had forced us to write, they admitted extracting confessions of crimes I had not committed by illegal methods. The two officers invited me to be quite open about my prison experiences and asked me to state whether I felt innocent or not, and what proof I could produce in case I desired rehabilitation.

I typed a long statement for them, this time on my own. At first, I thought it best to be very careful and mention only my innocence and the methods used to force my confession. But I knew that this would be telling a lie, and I decided to risk telling the whole truth.

I began with my deposition regarding Slansky and stated that Gottwald must have known of Slansky's innocence. I stated that the entire party leadership and government must have known that all of the defendants in my trial were innocent, and that it was actually the party's own governmental policy that was declared criminal, not my codefendants and I. I also mentioned my conflict with Mikoyan and his role in my imprisonment.

After reading my statement, both of the officers seemed favorably impressed and promised me a transfer to a more comfortable prison while further investigations were made. As it turned out, I had taken a risk and lost.

This statement of mine coupled with my behavior in prison—I had taken part in a hunger strike and a prision revolt and openly criticized the establishment—may have been responsible for what followed. Whereas my two surviving codefendants, Hajdu and London, were released and rehabilitated in 1956, shortly after

Khrushchev revealed Stalin's and Beria's crimes, I had to wait four more years to be released. Even then, my release was the result of a general pardon, and I was put on probation for some time afterward. In the meantime, the "comfortable" prison I was transferred to turned out to be a concentration camp.

Kohoutek and Doubek were sentenced to eight years, but they were released after two. Meanwhile, I, their victim, remained in prison for two years beyond their release. Still, prison life had some redeeming aspects and could not be compared with solitary confinement.

I met a great number of first-rate people and made many friends; a feeling of solidarity developed among the political prisoners, even if they differed in their political outlooks. There was an incredible intellectual ferment, with discussions among the available experts ranging from nuclear physics to philosophy and economics. I wish I could find a similar intellectual climate and general intellectual curiosity on university campuses today.

Khrushchev had embraced Tito at Belgrade Airport, and American and West German tourists crowded the expensive hotels in Prague, but essentially nothing changed in the routine of my life. I was moved from camp to camp, from prison to prison. Sometimes I was in solitary confinement; at other times, I shared a cell, with former Communists, lunatics, thieves, Catholics— even with a man called Sano Mach, one of the top collaborators with the Nazis, the very man who sent Slovak Jews into the furnaces of the Nazi concentration camps.

After eight years in prison, my life was ruled by routine. I went from job to job, from meals to exercise periods, from my cell to the prison workshop, a sleepwalker oblivious to my surroundings and living only from one day to the next. The only breaks in my routine were the letters I received from my wife and son and their visits four times a year. They had to travel eighteen hours by train from Bohemia to one of the Slovak prisons in which I was incarcerated. They saw me for forty-five minutes and then traveled eighteen hours back.

They always tried to smile and show an optimistic face, but I understood how hard it was for them just to survive. All apartments in Socialist countries were being allotted through official papers called "decrees." Relatives of a traitor could naturally not get a decree for an apartment of their own, so my wife and Ivan had to live in sublets. It was difficult to find people courageous enough to take them in, and some of the places they were forced to take were run-down and almost unlivable.

Only later, when the government introduced cooperative housing so that tenants could own their apartments after they had repaid the building costs, was my wife able to find a comfortable home. My mother-in-law in Austria sent her enough money to buy an apartment of her own. For a sum in Western currency, even the family of a traitor could find a place to live.

In April of 1960, an officer of the security service ordered me to pack my belongings and took me to the storeroom where the prisoners' civilian clothing was kept. I recognized mine at once: everything was neatly pressed, even the underwear, but time had reduced my shirt and pants to rags.

Nevertheless, I was pleased. I could not help thinking that I was going to be released. For weeks there had been rumors that a general pardon would be declared on May 9 in celebration of the fifteenth anniversary of the liberation of Czechoslovakia from Nazi occupation. In her last letter, Fritzi had also hinted that there might be such a pardon. I was very impatient. After eleven years in prison, if they were going to set me free, I wanted to be freed quickly.

One hour later, two other officers came to the storeroom and told me to empty my pockets. I had only a pipe, some tobacco, and a pipe cleaner, but they were very strict and made me hand them over.

They took me out into the prison yard, handcuffed me, and put me into the back seat of a black limousine, between two plainclothes policemen. A uniformed policeman was driving.

I did not know what to think: they were plainclothesmen, yet I was handcuffed. On the other hand, I was not being taken in the usual prison bus. We were driving toward Prague. Awakened from my lethargy, I wavered between ecstasy one minute and desperation the next.

When we entered the outskirts of the city, I could see that we were driving toward the airport. I was going back to Ruzyne, back to the place where I had begun my life as a prisoner.

When we reached the prison, I was put into one of the cells used for solitary confinement, but they did not order me to change my clothes. Since I was not issued a uniform, I knew that I was not going to be interviewed or taken to court. I was now sure that I was going to be released and that they were holding me there until they could prepare the necessary papers.

I decided to test my theory with a trick. I knocked on the cell door and shouted for the guard. When he came, I told him that I wanted something to read. I figured he would either give me hell for asking for a book, or grant my request. When he returned a few minutes later with a worn copy of Goethe's *Faust,* I was sure that it was only a matter of time until I would be released.

It was already night, but I was too excited to fall asleep. I smoked one pipe after another, thinking about what it would be like to be free again, hardly daring to believe that after so long my nightmare would be over.

At about four o'clock in the morning, they woke me up and led me to the prison yard. There was a bus waiting, one of those long, special prisoner-transport buses with small cells along the corridor and barely enough room to move. They took my shoes away, handcuffed me, and loaded me into one of the small cells. There was no window, and I had no idea in which direction we were going. After an hour or so, I could tell that we were out of the city and on an open road.

Two hours later, a guard unlocked the door and asked me if I needed to use the toilet; there was a small lavatory in one of the bus's cells for that purpose. He gave me a cup of coffee and a piece of bread.

He returned with more bread and coffee at noon, and then again that evening. I was locked in that small cell for eighteen hours, and every part of my body ached. By the time we reached our destination late at night, my spirits were very low; I could hear the clanging of heavy doors and the guards on our bus reporting to the guards of a new prison.

The guards on the bus spoke Czech, but I could hear the guards outside answer in Slovak; I knew I was in Slovakia.

They took me from the bus to a clothing storeroom. There are two kinds of prison dress: the regular uniform, and a special one for prisoners under interrogation, which has no belt or buttons. The officer in charge took my civilian clothes and handed me the uniform for prisoners under interrogation.

They led me down several long corridors to the part of the prison reserved for solitary confinement and put me in a large cell with three beds. I was the only prisoner.

No one came to see me that day, and when I asked to see an officer, the guard ignored me. I thought about starting a hunger strike, but I decided that it might be better to wait a few days. And then, two days later, a guard came and took me back to the storeroom.

"There has been a mistake," the officer in charge said. "Change your clothes. You aren't going to be interrogated."

I put my ordinary uniform on again and was taken back to my cell. Now things had become even more mysterious. If I was just an ordinary prisoner, why was I being isolated? I had already spent more than five years in solitary confinement; why was I alone again? A wave of desperation and helplessness overwhelmed me. What was going on, and why?

It was Sunday, and I had been in this Slovak prison for a week. I was sitting on my bed and staring into space when I heard footsteps approaching through the corridor toward my cell.

A guard opened the door, and two high-ranking security officers entered the cell. One of them asked, "You are Eugen Loebl?"

I came to attention and said that I was.

He stiffened and said in a slow, solemn voice: "Today, on the fifteenth anniversary of the liberation of our country by the glorious Red Army, the President of the Czechoslovak Socialist Republic has declared a general pardon."

When he finished, he looked down at his shoes and then back at me, as if he expected me to say something. Then he asked, "Would you like to know what the pardon covers?"

I said that I would.

The officer took a folded piece of paper from the breast pocket of his uniform, unfolded it with great ceremony, and read it to me. As he listed the crimes covered by the clemency, it became clear that I would be one of those pardoned. Now, after eleven years, I would be free.

"You will be released tomorrow morning, Loebl."

They turned and left the cell, and the guard locked the door behind them.

Now something strange happened. I did not feel any elation, or even any happiness. I had been desperately waiting for the moment when those eleven endless years would end, and now, face to face with life outside, I was unsure.

Besides, the pardon did not mean that I was declared innocent. Legally I was still a traitor, and I could and would be discriminated against in everything I did. And the pardon was only conditional: if I committed the smallest crime or infraction of the law, I would have to return to prison to serve my regular sentence.

The next morning, after a shave and a haircut, I put on civilian dress once again. My heart beat fast, but instead of taking me to the gates, they took me to another room and gave me a declaration to sign. It stated that I would under no circumstances and to no one reveal the nature of my interrogation, of my trial, or of my prison experience. In case of any indiscretion, I would be arrested at once, put on trial, and returned to prison.

After giving me back my few possessions, they took me out into the prison yard, where a car was waiting. As we passed through the gate, I recognized that we were in Bratislava, the capital of Slovakia.

Again I was sitting in the back seat next to a policeman, and there was another policeman driving. The one sitting next to me gave the driver the address of my family. I remember that I just sat there in the seat, a mass of swelling, still-unbelieving joy.

When we stopped in front of the house where my wife had her apartment, one of the policemen helped me out of the car. I was like a drunk in a stupor, moving like a zombie up the stairs and into the house.

As in a grade-B picture, my wife was just about to leave the apartment when she saw me. She let out a cry. We embraced.

"This is my wife," I told the policeman, holding her tightly to me.

The policeman played his part until the end.

"Mrs. Loebl, I have brought you back your husband."

The incredible had happened: I was not in prison any more; I was home. I was in a nice apartment with a kitchen, a room for my son, which was filled with books and a seemingly endless number of insects, my wife's room, which was elegantly furnished and contained a television set, and even a room for me. The apartment was full of beautiful antique furniture, which was cheap and easy to obtain in Slovakia.

My son was at work. He had a job in a museum about thirty miles from the city. As the son of a traitor to the state, he had not been permitted to go to college, but in spite of that, he was managing to pursue his vocation. He had already written and published a number of scientific papers in journals at home and abroad, and he was not at all bitter about what had happened to him because of me. And I was also happy to see that in no instance had Ivan compromised himself to try to compensate to the party for his relationship to me.

We had endless talks, acquainting each other with the years we had spent apart, the separate worlds in which we had lived. I saw Ivan listening with interest to my theories, and I was deeply impressed with his devotion to his mother. Her health broken by jail and forced labor, Fritzi would not have survived without his help, or without the money and parcels that her parents had been sending her from abroad. Chocolate, coffee, and tea could be sold advantageously at black-market prices, and cigarettes could be used to bribe shop assistants in state stores, to get items that were otherwise not available or available only after waiting in endless lines. Thanks to those parcels from her parents and Ivan's devotion to her, Fritzi was relatively well off.

A stream of visitors came to our apartment that first day and had many warm words for me. Fritzi told me that quite a few of them had kept their distance a few years back, when my situation was completely hopeless. She could understand why, but she could not forgive them.

The next morning, I went to the local police station to get a new identity card, and then to the office of the Ministry of Labor, where an official who was in charge of handling cases like mine told me that I would be working in a nearby bread factory as a manual laborer. I was to report to work in ten days.

Less than a week after my release from prison, I suffered a heart attack. Fearing complications, I spent part of each day during my recuperation putting on paper the theories I had committed to memory during my time in solitary confinement. Sentence by sentence I transcribed the book from memory; by the time I was discharged from the hospital, I had a complete manuscript.

So there I was, almost a citizen. But adjusting to life "outside" was not as simple as obtaining a job and an identity card; my prison routine was not so easily broken. I still woke up at six o'clock every morning; my stomach expected lunch at twelve o'clock; at four o'clock, wherever I was, I saw myself walking in the prison yard with the other prisoners; and at six o'clock in the evening, I had dinner with them in my thoughts. I had nightmares about being in prison, mostly that I was locked in a cell and they would not let me out. To be sure, prison life was still part of me.

There were other problems. I looked at Fritzi, courageous in spite of her exhaustion, trying hard to keep up an illusion of love. She had stuck with me for eleven years, suffered because of me, followed me across the country from prison to prison. She had made me feel her love in my prisoner's booth; she had reached through the wire mesh with her understanding and steadfastness.

But now, as we faced each other in the same apartment—in her apartment—I realized that this bond between us had loosened. Now that I was free and no longer needed her help, she felt, possibly in spite of herself, that she was a separate, independent being.

She had succeeded during those difficult years in supporting herself and in giving our son the education he needed. Standing in as mother and father while trying to make a living before the parcels from Austria were permitted to come in, she had survived on her own.

Because of Fritzi's newly acquired strength, I felt like an intruder who was interfering with her independence. We had lived through all those years under such different conditions that each of us had developed an independent personality. Our relationship had changed, and deep inside, I knew we were going to part.

The world that I now faced was very different from the one I had imagined in prison. Through my contact with hundreds of "freshman" prisoners during the past years, I thought I had learned a lot about what was going on in Czechoslovakia and the world at large. But the reality that confronted me at my release did not correspond to my image.

I spoke to many people, friends both old and new. Most of them were party members, but there were also some who had been expelled from the party and persecuted, or at least discriminated against; there were even some who had never been in the party. I was surprised to find very little difference among them in political views. All of them spoke about the party and the whole regime with contempt and even hatred.

One of my friends was a journalist for a party paper. When I met him one day, I told him that I strongly disagreed with an article of his I had just read, which supported some of the government's policies. He smiled at me and replied that he disagreed with it even more. But, he explained, he was a journalist and had to write according to the party line. If he did not, he would lose his job and be forced to work as a manual laborer.

Slowly it became clear to me that lying was now a way of life. Parents did not talk openly in front of their children. At meetings, or in the presence of strangers, people expressed one view, and among friends they expressed another, usually the opposite. No one considered this immoral; no one felt that he was forced to behave in such a manner. It was simply the normal way of life; anyone who said outright what he really thought was regarded as a fool.

It was all so strange to me. The years of Stalinist persecution were over; people were no longer imprisoned for their views. But to remain a white-collar worker, to stay in a slightly higher-paying job, one had to follow the rules; one had to toe the party line. I began to feel that everybody struggling to survive in the system was, in a sense, less free than we prisoners had been.

The working class was supposed to be the ruling class, and, consequently, everyone in a blue-collar job tried to make a career for himself as a white-collar worker. But, at the same time, the white-collar workers were afraid to become members of the ruling class. It made no sense.

I was also struck by the incredible amount of corruption which permeated every facet of society. If you wanted a better quality of meat, fruit, or shoes, you had to bribe the shopkeeper, with a few cigarettes at least, to get it. For Western cigarettes or a bottle of vodka, you could obtain better treatment or better medicine from your physician. The seller's market and consequent corruption extended even to the industrial level: if a nationalized factory wanted some deliveries made from another nationalized factory, the buyer had to bribe the selling official.

The economic situation of the country was appalling. Nothing functioned. The housewives who had to spend all their free time going from shop to shop to find what they needed became the most vocal opposition, but they had to be careful to blame only the shopkeeper, not the party.

In some ways, life outside of prison was just as bad as life inside. Almost no one was permitted to travel abroad, especially to the West. Only the most reliable party members, or those who had very good connections with powerful officials, were allowed to leave the country. I began to feel that I had come from a prison with walls to a prison without them. The Iron Curtain was invisible, but very effective.

I learned that, in 1956, there had been a short period of hope after Khrushchev revealed Stalin's and Beria's crimes. A few of the victims of the political trials had been released and rehabilitated, and writers had begun to criticize party policies. But the control exercised by the Stalinist regime was carried on by the neo-Stalinists, though in a much more subtle way. Now there was neither brutal persecution nor freedom; simply a colorless monotony.

I became a manual laborer and began to see society from the bottom instead of from the top; as a pardoned traitor on probation, I could not even enjoy the limited rights of a normal citizen. I soon found, however, that my fellow workers did not care at all about my past. They were not interested in whether I had been a traitor or not; the important thing was how well I worked.

I also discovered that the workers were the one group that did not lie: they said what they thought. And why not? They had nothing to lose; as blue-collar workers, they could not be degraded or demoted to a lower job. They despised the party, the government, and the intellectuals, but their concern was not with freedom of the press, of art, or of political expression. They focused on the payroll.

Bratislava is just a few miles from the Austrian border, and Austrians often came to visit the city. In this way, the working-class Slovaks learned that the Austrian workers were paid far more for less work than they were, and they felt even more exploited than those who worked for the capitalists. While the Slovaks did not want a return to capitalism, they did want at least the same wages and the same standard of living that capitalism had achieved.

Most of the workers I talked to actually did oppose a return to private ownership of the means of production. But they were not really interested in the politics of the system, as long as they could have at least the same pay as the workers in capitalist countries received.

In prison, everything had seemed so simple. The guards were on one side, and the prisoners were on the other. And the guards were real. We felt their power and ruthlessness, and we could hate them outright and tell them what we thought of them. The establishment was tangible in prison, and, personified by the guards, it was an object for our condemnation.

But in the "free" world of the civilian, party and government were abstract concepts. Everyone knew that his fate depended on the party, for a shift in the party line meant a change in society and in the lives of its people. But it was difficult to personify this invisible force which could affect you at will; there was no object to strike out at. In privacy, people criticized or disliked or hated the party, but it was the same as criticizing the weather or a disease: no matter what happened, you were powerless against it, a helpless victim.

There had been clear division lines in prison. We were able to distinguish between those who were willing to cooperate with the guards, for whatever reason, and those who refused any kind of cooperation. In the prison without walls that was the outside world, everyone tried to cooperate in order to improve his position, or at least maintain it. A citizen had his family to protect, as well as his privacy and personal interests, and only a few were so concerned with values that they would dare to act according to them.

As a result of all this, people naturally felt that they were simply objects, depersonalized and manipulated by the government; we had felt the same way in prison. Also like us, they longed for freedom, for a dignified life, and for a humane society. But there was a single important difference between us.

My fellow prisoners and I believed that our situation could change for the better. We had to believe this in order to survive, and we were able to believe it because the very limitations of the world we had access to gave us the hope that there was an "outside" that might restore our freedom and dignity. In contrast, most of the people I met in my civilian life did not believe that things could change or that those in power could be overwhelmed. It is impossible to take any effective action for change without this faith. And there is the broader, graver question of whether people conditioned not to believe in their own effectuality can produce any real change in society even if they are motivated by a vision of a better future.

Who knows the answer? From my experience in both worlds, I can only say that it is far more difficult to nourish a belief in change and a desire to act in a gray, depressed, wholly pragmatic and manipulated world than it was even in the solitary confinement of a prison cell.

Postscript

In the three years following my liberation, the political situation in Czechoslovakia gradually changed. It began with a dispute between factions within the Politburo. The economy had declined, and the economic policies of the party First Secretary and President of the Republic, Antonin Novotny, had alienated a significant number of high-level officials. Because Novotny defended Stalinism in general and the rigid controls of a Soviet-model "planned" economy, he came under increasing attack from a group of reformers within the party apparatus who supported less centralized control of every aspect of the economy.

The dispute was intensified by another split: the long-standing division between the two nationality groups that make up Czechoslovakia, the Czechs and the Slovaks, each with their own culture and language. The pro-Stalinist Novotny wing was dominated by Czechs and consciously discriminated against Slovaks. There was particularly strong criticism of the First Secretary of the Slovak Communist party, Karel Bacilek, who was not himself a Slovak. As former head of the state security apparatus and a close associate of Novotny, he had made numerous enemies in the party leadership. Bacilek's dismissal led to the elevation of Alexander Dubcek to the post of first secretary of Slovakia, and the reformers soon found in Dubcek a valuable ally.

It was this conflict within the Politburo that actually triggered the beginning of a revolution that was to lead to the liberated climate of the "Prague Spring," and its suppression by the invasion of the Soviet and satellite armies.

I think it can be accepted as a rule that any great changes, even revolutionary changes, in countries under the dictatorship of Communist parties start with conflicts within the Politburo. Once the monolith shows some signs of cracks, the forces of the opposition find space to express themselves. It was so in Poland, when Gomulka came to power, in Hungary when Nagy came to power, and even in the Soviet Union when Khrushchev came to power.

One of the most important features of the breakdown of the monolith in Czechoslovakia was the role played by the intelligentsia. Writers, philosophers, historians, social scientists, artists, journalists, and others expressed their oppositional views and became the intellectual leaders of the majority of the nation, which was very open to honest critical views. A new revolutionary intellectual climate developed. No barricades, no violence, no persecution—intellectual weapons alone accomplished a genuine revolution. The revolution of the intellectuals became an intellectual revolution. It penetrated everywhere, even into the party apparatus, among many typical apparatchiks including those in the Central Committee and the Politburo. Dubcek, in his conflict with President Novotny, opened this avenue, and very soon was carried by the wave of desire to create a society, a Socialism with a human face.

Most astonishing and encouraging was the reaction of high-school and university students. Although they had been exposed from elementary school on to the official Marxist philosophy and had practically been brainwashed, they were the most sensitive group in the country to liberated views and humanistic ideals, and they became one of the most militant forces for a genuine humanistic society.

The urge to create a new society based on Socialism with a human face became a uniting force for all strata, creeds, and world views, and sponsored the Prague Spring. Interestingly, the least enthusiastic stratum was the proletariat.

I did not know Dubcek personally until after he became first secretary of the Slovak party. I knew that he had made his career during the height of Stalinism in Czechoslovakia, that he had been brought up in the Soviet Union, and that he was a very loyal apparatchik. I had heard him speak at meetings and read some of his articles and was struck only by the fact that he used the most boring, stereotyped, party-approved language.

I met him for the first time in the spring of 1963, when he summoned me to his office. At the time, there were already rumors that the purge trials were being re-examined and that some of the defendants would be rehabilitated. I thought that Dubcek was going to give me official notice of my rehabilitation.

He was in his early forties then, a slim man with a handsome face and a warm smile. I do not remember the color of his eyes, for it was not their color that struck me, but their kindness.

I found his good nature the more impressive because I had never expected a first secretary who had advanced his career under Stalinism to be so personable; it seemed like a deviation from the party line.

He told me that the party leadership had asked him to head a committee to look into the Clementis case and mine. He had read a report by foreign-trade experts which concluded unanimously that my conduct in the negotiations was not criminal and had not harmed the Republic. They agreed, furthermore, that I had handled a difficult situation in the best possible way. Then he told me he had read the confessions of Doubek and Kohoutek and the deposition I wrote in 1956. There were tears in Dubcek's eyes. He held my arm and could hardly speak. He asked me to believe him when he said that he had never imagined that such horrors were being perpetrated by the party. Now that he knew the truth, he spent sleepless nights wondering how he could have made a career through such a regime. He was glad that, in my case at least, some of the harm might yet be undone, but he was shaken by the cruel fate of Clementis, a man he had always admired.

We spoke at length about the injustice of the trials, and not once did Dubcek look at them from a strictly "political" point of view. Nor did he mention any political or pragmatic reasons for them. He appeared to me to be a simple, honest, and decent human being. Never addressing me as the powerful first secretary who had my fate in his hands, Dubcek spoke as a fellow human being, sincerely sympathetic for the victims of the trials.

Perhaps I am wrong, or biased, but I had the feeling that what Dubcek had read about the party's treatment of defendants during the trials had a strong impact on the development of his humanistic policies after he became first secretary of the national Communist party in the beginning of 1968.

I saw him again, immediately after his promotion, at his first meeting with representatives of the farmers. He began his speech by saying in a trembling voice, "I bow my head before your callused hands." It was the same voice and the same expression he had had when he spoke of his horror over the cruelty of the trials.

In my opinion, Dubcek's honesty, sincerity, and humanity were important in encouraging a national movement based on humanistic ideals, for his very personality exemplified commitment to such values.

Dubcek ended his 1963 meeting with me by informing me that in a matter of weeks I would be officially rehabilitated by the Czechoslovak Supreme Court and the party.

Restored to full political rights, I was appointed economic adviser to the Ministry of Foreign Trade, with the rank of deputy minister. I used my rehabilitation to contribute to *Kulturny Zivot,* the weekly journal of the Slovak Writers Union. My articles openly challenged the basic assumptions of Marxism and even criticized the reformers for not having the courage to reject Stalin's ideological and philosophical roots along with the Stalinist political system. The Central Committee of the party responded by formally condemning my conclusions and denying me the promised position in the ministry. Instead I was sent to Bratislava to be director of the State Bank of Slovakia.

But it was no longer possible for them to persecute me, or even to forbid me to publish my views. I took advantage of this new climate by having the manuscript I had "written" in prison published by the Slovak Academy of Sciences. It appeared in 1967, under the title *Mental Work: The True Source of Wealth.* A year later I published an account of the political background and methods that produced the Slansky trials. It became a best seller in Czechoslovakia and was subsequently published in eight European countries, in Japan, and in the United States (under the title *Stalinism in Prague*).

With the Prague Spring it seemed that Stalinism in Czechoslovakia was dead. The new developments left me in the unexpected position of having published my theories, having those theories favorably received by many in the country, and being in line to become minister of foreign trade after the Czechoslovak party congress that was scheduled for September 1968.

But that party congress, which was slated to approve basic changes in the party and Czechoslovak society, was never held. The power of humanistic ideals had transcended the borders of Czechoslovakia, threatening the Soviet leadership's control over the Eastern bloc and even over its own party. On August 21, 1968, less than a month before the planned party congress, Czechoslovakia was occupied by the Warsaw Pact armies. What had begun as a rejection of Stalinism ended with the suppression of a national movement for humanism. With the reimposition of Stalinism during the Soviet occupation, events had come full circle.

After the Soviet occupation of Czechoslovakia, Dr. Gustav Husak, my former student, fellow prisoner, and lifelong friend, and at that time deputy prime minister (now first secretary of the Communist party and president of the Republic), decided to accept Brezhnev's policy of establishing absolute control over Czechoslovakia. I refused his invitation to do likewise and chose exile in the West.

I settled in Austria and wrote an analysis of the Prague Spring, *The Intellectual Revolution,* which was published in Austria and

Germany. In this analysis I concluded that the revolution in the West would have to be an intellectual one, a complete rethinking of all the concepts on which the Western socioeconomic model is based.

I accepted an invitation to attend a "Symposium on the Impact of the U.S.A. on the World" at Princeton and subsequently lectured at more than twenty-five universities throughout the United States. Fascinated by the response I got, particularly among university students, to the idea of a society based on humane values, I decided to stay in this country. I accepted a teaching position, first at Southern Illinois University and then at Vassar College, where my teaching is actually based on the insights I gained in solitary confinement. Although I shared my students' enthusiasm to create a new and better world, I was most disturbed to see that their "progressive" and "revolutionary" movement was based on outdated theories. The attempt to solve the problems of the most highly developed country in the world by the application of the theories of Marx and Engels, who were thinkers of the past century, or even those of Mao or Ho Chi Minh, who were dealing with the social and economic problems of countries that were still in the stage of the industrial revolution, can only become self-destructive. I wrote *Conversation with the Bewildered,* in which I tried to communicate my experience in Czechoslovakia. The book, first published in Germany and then in Great Britain and the U.S.A., appeared when the radicals had already destroyed their movement and a deep disillusionment and apathy had replaced the enthusiasm of the sixties.

The new wave of interest in Marxism led me to write *Marxism: Thoroughfare or Dead End,* published in Germany and Austria and now being translated into Italian, French, and English. In this book I tried to show that the developed world is facing a crisis different from anything Marx witnessed, and that the very failure of applied Marxism in the East could provide valuable lessons for the Western left.

The problems of a mature society cannot be solved by Marx, Engels, and their reformers, or by the teachings of the classics of capitalism and *their* modest reformers. The deep social, economic, political, and human crisis of the seventies has been ample proof of that, as well as a challenge to find new avenues. My application to a mature society of the conclusions I reached in solitary confinement has been published in my *Humanomics.*